CYBERSECURITY 101
A DUMMY'S GUIDE FOR BEGINNERS

L.D. KNOWINGS

Copyright © 2024 L.D. Knowings. All rights reserved.

The content within this book may not be reproduced, duplicated, or transmitted without direct written permission from the author or the publisher.

Under no circumstances will any blame or legal responsibility be held against the publisher, or author, for any damages, reparation, or monetary loss due to the information contained within this book, either directly or indirectly.

Legal Notice:

This book is copyright protected. It is only for personal use. You cannot amend, distribute, sell, use, quote, or paraphrase any part of the content within this book, without the consent of the author or publisher.

Disclaimer Notice:

Please note the information contained within this document is for educational and entertainment purposes only. All effort has been expended to present accurate, up-to-date, reliable, and complete information. No warranties of any kind are declared or implied. Readers acknowledge that the author is not engaged in the rendering of legal, financial, medical, or professional advice. The content within this book has been derived from various sources. Please consult a licensed professional before attempting any techniques outlined in this book.

By reading this document, the reader agrees that under no circumstances is the author responsible for any losses, direct or indirect, that are incurred as a result of the use of the information contained within this document, including, but not limited to, errors, omissions, or inaccuracies.

CONTENTS

Introduction	7
1. FOUNDATION OF CYBERSECURITY	13
Network Security and Their Various Type	15
Endpoint Security Essentials	18
Endpoint Security Best Practices	21
Understanding Threats and Vulnerabilities	26
How to Recognize Potential Vulnerability	29
Key Cybersecurity Concept	31
2. SECURING THE CLOUDS AND APPLICATIONS	33
Exploring Cloud Security Fundamentals	33
Why Cloud Security is Different from Traditional Data Storage	34
Basic Cloud Security Measures	37
Strategies to Secure Cloud Environment and Data	40
Importance of Personal Responsibility in Cloud Security	45
World Examples of Cloud Security Breaches and They Could Have Been Prevented	45
Basics of Application Security in Software Development	46
Some Guidelines for Choosing and Using Secured Applications Daily	47
Personal Security Audit	48
3. IDENTITY, ACCESS, AND ENCRYPTION	51
Comprehensive View of Identity and Access Management (IAM)	51
The Importance of Strong IAM Strategies to Prevent Unauthorized Access	52
Tips for Managing Digital Identities and Access Controls	53
The Role of Cryptography in Cybersecurity	54
Roles of Encryption in Protecting Data	55

Common Encryption Methods and their Applications	56
Best Practices for Authentication, Authorization, and Data Encryption	57
Tips on How to Encrypt Personal Data and the Importance of Using Encryption in Various Online Activities	59
Data Encryption Plan Worksheet:	60
4. RESPONDING TO CYBERSECURITY INCIDENTS	**65**
Detailed Approach to Incident Response and Management	65
Steps for Preparing and Responding to Cybersecurity Incident	67
Tips on Initial Action to Take Immediately After Discovering a Breach	68
Importance of Communication During an Incident	71
Steps to Communicate Effectively With Stakeholders	72
Steps to Communicate Internally During a Cybersecurity Incident	74
Case Study of Effective Incident Response	76
Cloud Service Template: Quick Thinking and Effective Planning	77
Quiz:	77
5. GOVERNANCE, COMPLIANCE, AND RISK MANAGEMENT	**79**
Understanding Security Governance Framework	79
The Role and Importance of a Framework in Shaping an Organization's Cybersecurity Strategy	81
Popular Framework and their Fundamental Principles	81
Compliance with Cybersecurity Laws and Regulations	84
Cybersecurity Laws and Regulations	86
Tips to Stay Updated With Changing Laws and Regulations	87
Techniques for Managing Cybersecurity Risks	87
Importance of Risk Management in Cybersecurity	88
Risk assessment methodologies and their applications	89

| The Methodologies | 89 |
| Creating a Risk Management Plan | 93 |

6. SECURING THE INTERNET OF THINGS (IOT) — 95
Challenges and Solutions in IoT Security	95
How to Mitigate These Vulnerabilities	98
Real-world Incidents Where IoT Devices Were Compromised	100
Methods to Protect Interconnected Devices	101
The Importance of Regular Software Updates and Strong Network Security Practices	103
The Role of User Awareness and Behavior in IoT Security	104
Future Trends in IoT Cybersecurity	105
Future Challenges and Opportunities in IoT Security	108
Quiz	109

7. THREAT INTELLIGENCE AND PROACTIVE DEFENSE — 111
Exploring Cyberthreat Intelligence	111
Types of Threat Intelligence	113
Importance of Understanding Threat Landscape	114
Real-life Examples of Threat Intelligence Operations	114
Techniques and Tools for Cyber Threat Hunting	115
Standard Tools and Techniques Used in Threat Hunting	116
More Cyber threat hunting tools:	119
Tips for Basic Threat Hunting Practices	121
Building a Proactive Cybersecurity Strategy	123
How to Incorporate Threat Intelligence into Daily Cybersecurity Practices	124
Continuous Nature of Cybersecurity	124
Crosswords	125
Emerging Trends and Technologies	126
Evolution of Cyber Threat	133
Importance of Staying Informed about New Technologies for Effective Cybersecurity	138
Predictions for the Future Challenges in Cybersecurity:	139
How Current Trends Might Evolve and Impact Cybersecurity Strategies	139

The Importance of Adaptability and Continuous
Learning in the Face of These Challenges   140
Preparing for the Evolving Cyber Threat Landscape   141

Conclusion   143
References   147

INTRODUCTION

What comes to your mind on hearing breaking news about a significant data breach in, let's say, a giant social media network? Undoubtedly, you will be anxious thinking about the safety of your data. You're not alone in this; many people would do the same. The security of our cyberspace continues to be an essential discussion in our technological world. More than ever, it has become a more relevant topic of conversation today. The advent of computers and the internet has been an excellent achievement for man and industry. It is central to the third industrial revolution.

The good news is that our cyberspace has become more advanced than it was in the past century with the speed of the internet, almost seamless data synchronization across various departments and organizations, swift transactions, and innovative governance across multiple sectors and industries. All these have transformed our lives and offered new exploration opportunities. But there exist forces that threaten the tremendous progress made so far and even hinder us from the many other options- cyber threats.

Cybercriminals are relentless in their pursuit to find their next victim and exploit their vulnerability to maximum advantage. They leave their poor victims in pain, regret, agony, and huge losses. Not one is immune to the snares of these criminals unless you're conscious of their threats and take proactive steps towards clipping their wings while enjoying the benefits of cyberspace. This is where cybersecurity comes in, and you need to be aware and take charge of your cybersecurity.

The technical nature of cybersecurity makes it overwhelming to grasp the simple details and even more confusing to understand if you're not vast in the science of computers. The limited understanding of cybersecurity puts users in perpetual fear of possible threats whenever they are online or offline. The news about failed cybersecurity systems and data breaches causes anxiety among users due to the fear of falling victim to the activities of hackers. Every day, more devices are churned out of factories to meet the ever-changing needs of the end users. Good enough, some manufacturers have carefully considered the cyber threats of their devices, making them develop improved devices that can easily allow users to fortify their security in cyberspace. However, keeping up with the upgrades on these devices is another challenge for users, and keeping up with the pace can take time and effort. Work-life, especially for users, is stressful enough and leaves users with little or no time to keep up with new and emerging trends that can allow them to implement cybersecurity best practices, thereby making cybersecurity provisions in these devices ineffective due to either ignorance or the difficulty to understand some of the technicalities involved to activate the security features in these devices against any potential cyber threats. Data-hungry applications and websites that spice up our day and make life easier are also points of concern, and putting a balance between our convenience and how much of our data can be given out and its security can be a tough choice.

But before attempting to go any further, you need to understand what network and endpoint security are to fully appreciate and implement what you will learn in this book. First, when discussing network security, we look at the tools, techniques, and policies that allow you to prevent misuse, modification, or unauthorized access to your network with its resources. Your network can be a cloud-based, local area network (LAN), or a vast area network. However, you must know that network security involves several layers of protection, like switches, authentication, routers, monitoring, and encryption. These protection layers can help you secure your data from any unauthorized access in transit. It also lets you detect and block malicious traffic while enforcing compliance with existing standards and regulations.

On the other hand, endpoint security covers the tools, techniques, and policies employed to protect any device connected to your network. Devices such as PCs, laptops, servers, phones, and tablets. All these devices mentioned are endpoints, and they are mostly the points of entry into your network used by hackers to breach your valuable data assets and privacy. When talking about securing our endpoint or endpoint security, things like firewalls, encryption, patch management, backup, anti-malware, and antivirus are usually the focus because they help in data protection when not in use, removal of malware, and recovery in instances where you have a system failure or a crash.

The difference between network and endpoint security is straightforward and based on their scope of protection. While the former seeks to protect the network infrastructure and its perimeter, the latter deals with individual devices and their data. Network security is a defensive approach to prevent attacks from getting to the network. However, endpoint security is an offensive approach that can be taken to avoid attacks that limit the functionality of your devices. However, network and endpoint security protect and secure your systems and data. They are interdependent and complementary to each other.

Regarding cybersecurity, the network and endpoint security can benefit users immensely when implemented. Implementing network and endpoint security can reduce cybersecurity threats that may compromise your system, such as cyber-attacks, data breaches, and downtime. Also, it can help the performance and reliability of your devices and network. Generally, it improves the productivity and efficiency of your IT staff and users on the network while complying with the legal requirements and standards of your industry and its customers, which improves trust, reputation, and confidence in your business and brand.

Still, network security and endpoint security come with their various challenges. It would be best if you were constantly updated about emerging trends and vulnerabilities, able to manage diversities and complexities, balance usability and safety, and designate budget and resources for furnishing staff and users with knowledge on the best practices to overcome these challenges.

Everyone is at risk of a cybersecurity attack, and the consequences of a breach can be devastating; not even the tech giants are free from these threats. In April 2021, Facebook suffered a massive data breach that leaked data from over 500 million users to the public. This is another reason people must prioritize their security online and offline. However, technical issues, constant device upgrades, and lifestyle changes can pose huge setbacks. That is why you need a comprehensive guide to help you take charge of your cybersecurity, fortify your devices, and commit to safe internet usage without running into the trap of malicious hackers.

Although there are numerous guides, only some make it easier for users to understand the technicalities involved in cybersecurity. When they attempt to do so, the concepts are all the more complex and confusing. With all that, users find confronting the threat before them challenging, making them vulnerable in cyberspace. But I want something else for you. You should be able to understand the fundamentals of cybersecurity and use proactive steps to wade off any cyber threat and fortify your system. That is where this book comes in.

In this book, you will gain new insight and be able to develop a comprehensive plan to help you navigate the digital world. This book is like your companion who has all the tools to assist you in acquiring the necessities of cybersecurity without being bothered by all the technical jargon. Soon, this book will teach you how to identify and quickly prevent threats, guard your personal information, and bravely go about your online activities without hindrances. You will get practical tips and streamlined, implementable strategies that save time and energy. Take this book as a quick way to attain the status of a cyber-savvy individual who can protect oneself and be helpful to those around them in our ever-changing digital world. This book has much to bring you up to par in today's digital world. Whether it is understanding how to safeguard your home network, trying to figure out the fundamentals about privacy online, or managing passwords, this book would help you get there and break it down in a way that makes cybersecurity understandable and achievable.

As the author of this book, I understand the deepest concerns of users. I am determined to help them overcome these challenges. That is why I have carefully arranged chapters in this book to help readers keep up and follow the details. Also, I've written this book in a style that makes even the most complex concepts in the tech world comprehensible. You will get a few of these kinds of books out there. If you genuinely want to tackle the threat before you, the cybersecurity threat, and stay safe on the internet while using your devices, then this book is for you.

I have started this book with the basics, and you will see the foundations of cybersecurity. Then, you will notice how to secure your cloud and applications. You will also learn to identify, access, and encrypt and how to respond to cyber incidents when they occur. Later in the book, you will understand governance, compliance, and risk management about cybersecurity. It doesn't stop there; you will also learn how to secure the Internet of Things. Next are threat intelligence and proactive defense. Lastly, we will be taking a glance into the future of cybersecurity.

FOUNDATION OF CYBERSECURITY

Remember the last time your Internet was slow, and you wondered if it was just the wifi or something more sinister? That's where cybersecurity begins - in the ordinary moments of our digital lives. You may be confident with your assumptions, but again, there is a higher chance that something may be running in the background that you have probably yet to initiate. Something you're entirely oblivious about. It could be some applications or bugs that can run automatically, weighing down your internet speed or slowing down your system. You don't have to be a cybersecurity pro before you can tell what is happening. Or you decided to call upon a pro's attention to check what is going on. Assuming you're facing a threat, how long would it take before the cybersecurity pro arrives? Wouldn't the damage be done already? It would be best if you had profound thoughts on these questions. After that, you should understand reasons you should at least have the basics of these threats, even without being a pro. A foundation in cybersecurity should give you all the basics and position you to deal with any cyber threat as soon as you see a trace, helping you to operate safely in your network and secure your valuable data assets.

As you know, the foundation offers us the base upon which other structures are organized. The structures that form the foundation of cybersecurity are as follows:

Network Security Basics

Although I briefly discussed this in our introduction, let's delve deeper. As you must know, network security is all about protecting the underlying infrastructure of your network from misuse, breaches, or unauthorized access. It creates a safe infrastructure for users, their devices, and applications while carrying out various tasks.

How Network Security Works

Network Security works such that it pulls several layers of defenses from all corners, including from within the network. For every single security network layer, there is a corresponding policy and control to implement alongside it. This is so that those with authorization can successfully access the network. At the same time, those without and who want to come in through unauthorized means to gain access are blocked out. When these malicious actors are successfully blocked out of the network, their ability to carry out their preplanned threats and exploits diminishes.

The Benefits of Network Security

Today, our world has become digitalized at an unprecedented level. From how we live, play, work, interact, and even learn. Securing your network must be a top-notch priority if your business or employees offer services to people through the Internet. Doing so protects your organization's proprietary information from malicious attacks and your brand's reputation.

NETWORK SECURITY AND THEIR VARIOUS TYPE

Having seen what network security is and the benefits it offers, let's look into the various types of network security that exist:

Intrusion Prevention System(IPS)

This type of network security operates in the background, where it repeatedly scans through the network traffic to find any potential threats and block them accordingly. When using a secured IPS, you can rest assured that you have extra layers of protection. Secure IPS appliances correlate massive amounts of intelligence on global threats to contain all malicious traffic and track the progress of suspicious malware and files throughout the network to stamp out the spread of reinfecting the network or outbreak.

Firewalls

This type of network security offers devices that monitor traffic round the clock, whether the traffic is inbound or outwardbound. It decides what to do using its preprogrammed intelligent capabilities. This intelligence can block specific traffic or allow them to use defined rules. Firewalls are often the first line of defense called upon and have been in use for the past 25 years. They create a barrier between controlled and secured internal networks that are either trusted or untrusted outside the web, like the Internet. Firewalls can come in different forms: software, public cloud, hardware, private clouds, or software-as-a-service (SaaS).

Workload security

This type of network security protects the workloads moving in various hybrid environments and clouds. It is a way of breaking down your network to distribute the workloads and give a broader attack surface, giving an attacker more tasks on their plate. Still, these distributed workloads must be secured without weighing down on business outcomes.

Network segmentation

Here, software programs are used to segment and break down network traffic into different and smaller segments, making security policy enforcement easier. This classification is usually based on endpoint identity, not just an IP address. The right to access the network is assigned according to location and role to give the required access to the right people, while suspicious access is denied.

Secure X

This is yet another type of network security, and it is a cloud-native built into the platform that links your infrastructure and a secured Cisco portfolio. With it, you can cut down on time and human-controlled tasks.

Access control

Now, this type of network security allows access to only specific individuals. Everyone shouldn't have access to your network, and to have control of it, you must keep out attackers; you need to be able to identify each user and their devices to enforce your security measures effectively. You can allow only limited access or completely block noncompliant endpoint devices in Network Access Control (NAC).

VPN

A VPN stands for Virtual Private Network. It encrypts connections as they flow from one network point to where it terminates on the Internet. Your remote-access VPN uses Secure Sockets Layer or IPsec to authenticate the back-and-forth communication between networks and devices.

Antivirus and anti-malware software

The word malware is an acronym for "malicious software." Malicious attackers can use several kinds of malware to compromise your network. These malware are Trojans, spyware, worms, viruses, and Ransomware. Malware excitingly infects networks. When it infects a network, it may lie inactive for a couple of days, and the best form of anti-malware programs to counter these threats are those that not only scan your network when they detect an entry of malware but also repeatedly track scanned files to detect any abnormalities, remove the malware, repair the damage.

With antivirus packages, you can scan files or your computer memory for specific patterns that may tell that there is a presence of malicious software, and the antivirus looks for ways according to the signatures of established malware. Antivirus software vendors release new and updated malware regularly, and you must keep up with this update and affect it on your system.

ENDPOINT SECURITY ESSENTIALS

Behavioral analytics

Before talking about abnormal network behavior, you must understand the behavior of a typical network. With behavior analytics, you can determine whether an activity has deviated from the normal. With it, you can correctly identify the signs of compromise that could be a threat in the future and remediate the problem immediately.

Application security

Whatever software you subscribe to must be protected for personal or business use. It doesn't matter who the developer is, whether a trusted party or some random developer. It is because, most of the time, applications are not 100% safe, no matter their source; there are often vulnerabilities or loopholes that attackers can exploit to gain access to your network. When application security is mentioned, you should know I am talking about the hardware, software, and processes that prevent attackers from exploiting these loops.

Email security

Emails are popular gateways for most vector security breaches. The technique used by attackers is harvesting personal information coupled with social engineering strategies to develop phishing email campaigns to lure recipients and lead them to sites filled with malware. However, with a practical email security software application, you can block most incoming attacks while being in charge of outbound messages to avoid losing sensitive data.

Data Loss Prevention

Sensitive information must be strictly guarded to prevent leaks, and organizations must install software that prevents their staff from sending them outside the network. With data loss prevention technologies, you can stop anyone from printing, uploading, and forwarding sensitive information, especially in an insecure network.

Cloud Security

This type of network security involves a broad set of applications, technologies, and policies that can be used to protect online services, applications, and other essential data. It gives you better security management by defending against threats lurking anywhere and on the Internet when accessing it and safeguarding your applications and valuable data in the cloud.

Wireless Security

Wireless networks are more vulnerable than wired networks. So when choosing wireless, follow it up with fortifying security features. Installing your wireless LAN without that security measure means putting an Ethernet port anywhere, even at the public square. To avoid any form of exploitation, you must use your wireless alongside products that are dedicated to wireless network protection.

This type of network security allows you to control your employees' web use, deny access to dubious websites, and block any form of web-based threat. This way, you can protect your web gateways in the clouds or on-site. Web security is the measures you can take to prevent any potential attack on your website.

Security information and event management

This type of network security allows you to collect valuable information that your employees can use to detect and respond to threats adequately. Security information and event management products could come in a physical or virtual appliance or server software.

Mobile Device Security

Mobile devices and apps have become a lucrative target for most cybercriminals. In the next three years, 90 percent of IT organizations worldwide may need to support corporate applications on many personal mobile devices. With this threat level, controlling what devices should have access to your network is imperative. Also, to be safer, you must configure the network connection while keeping traffic private.

Industrial Network Security

A significant drawback in digitizing industrial operations and the deeper integration between industrial networks, cloud, and information technology(IT) is the vulnerability of the Industrial Control System to cyber threats. Here, it would be best to have better visibility into your operational technology or OT security outlook to segment your industrial network while feeding your IT security tools with enriched details on behaviors and OT devices.

ENDPOINT SECURITY BEST PRACTICES

This is yet another structure that forms the foundation of cybersecurity. Unlike network security, endpoint security is a frontline defense for individual devices. Take endpoint security as personal hygiene. In the same way, you protect your health by imbibing good habits, so you can also protect your devices with good cybersecurity practices. Endpoint security is a way or pattern of securing entry points or endpoints of consumer devices like mobile devices, laptops, and desktops from any vulnerabilities that attackers and their malicious campaigns can exploit. So, endpoint security systems protect those endpoints in the cloud or network from malicious cyberattacks. When talking about endpoint security, you should know that it has gone beyond the traditional antivirus software into all-around protection against evolving zero-day threats and complex malware.

No organization is spared from the risk of cyber threats, malicious and accidental insider threats to organized crime and hacktivists, or even nation-states. It will be in the right place if you consider endpoint security as a cybersecurity frontline, and it is often the first place where organizations look to provide needed protection for their business networks.

The scale and sophistication of cybersecurity continue to grow each day, and so does the need for more sophisticated endpoint security solutions. Brilliantly, the new endpoint protection systems are programmed to rapidly detect, analyze, block, or even deal with any active attack. But for this to happen, it must sync with other technologies to give administrators a comprehensive view of advanced threats to hasten detection and effect a quicker solution.

Some Tips for Endpoint Security Best Practices

1. Leave no room for exploitation by patching all devices and ensuring they're secure.

Before anything, you need to be sure that every device connected to your network is secured professionally, be it a laptop, printer, server, smartwatch, or mobile device. When these devices are allowed to access your enterprise network, then be sure you can track each of them, check for any connected new devices that want to connect to your network and update the endpoint inventory accordingly.

Take advantage of a software update or the most recent patch; upgrade your patch management policy as required. There may be drawbacks if all of these are done manually, so opt for an automated patching solution to keep you updated.

2. Strengthen your passwords.

If you build a house to keep thieves away from the inside, you need more robust doors. That is how password works. It is the doorway to access the inside of your network, and that must be made stronger for only those with the keys to go through. So, use passwords that cannot be easily guessed or manipulated. Combine your passwords with unique characters and ask users to generate and use complex passwords for their logins to prevent unauthorized access.

You can also activate a multifactor authentication solution to strengthen endpoint security even more.

3. Introduce the Principle of Least Privilege (PLP).

Introducing the principle of least privilege can help you mitigate the spread of potential infections before they get to every other part of the system. This way, you can reduce the losses of data and damage and identify and track how the breach happened and where it came from.

To save yourself from all the hassle, do not allow unauthorized users to install executable code into your endpoint, and you must strictly evaluate users who need admin privileges from those who don't.

4. Use encryption to secure endpoints.

For more fortified cybersecurity, use encryption to give an additional protection layer to your data. Always use encrypted memory or disk to secure information, even when it gets lost or stolen. That way, anyone who finds it other than you needs access to its information.

5. Implement a USB port access policy.

The most common way to spread malware or risk company data is through USB ports. Therefore, access to your USB ports should be fitted in the least-privilege policy to avoid any potential attack.

Even though their alternative access point makes USB less in use, hackers still need to key into their old tricks. Such an attack was on an endpoint using USB, which was in the spotlight after the Turla attack in Ukraine.

6. Employ VPN access for only remote endpoints.

With companies' increasing adoption of the hybrid or remote way of working, enforcing a VPN access policy becomes more than necessary. However, it doesn't protect your devices from DNS spoofing, DNS tunneling, Man-in-the-middle, and other external attacks. But you will be safer if you follow the VPN guidelines by limiting its use and only adopting it at the app layer.

Using a VPN, you can activate the multifactor authentication to keep your data safe.

7. Put in place a safe BYOD policy.

BYOD has become popular in recent years due to remote or hybrid work lifestyles. The more reason you need to have a second look at your internal security protocol.

If you must deal with BYOD safely, you need to enforce the guest account policy and fortify your defense through an additional fourth endpoint security practice I mentioned earlier. Encrypting endpoints will also protect users in situations of lost devices.

8. White/Blacklisting Apps

Remove all the things you don't need and leave only those you need. There is no point in keeping an app you don't require. So, there is no need to authorize its installation in the first place. It will reduce the risk of vulnerability to zero-day and other threats.

When you choose to allow access to an app, be sure to limit its communication possibilities to non-important segments.

9. Always go with the Zero Trust Security Model.

Don't trust; always double-check before using, and this is a rule that every user, app, workload, and endpoint access should allow only after a thorough check on one's identity and device. Then, apply the principle of least privilege and do so on all occasions. The principle of least privilege advocates for each user or device to have only the access they need to carry out the task.

To build a zero-trust policy, you need tools. It would be best to have network segmentation to isolate and prevent infection spreading, data usage controls, multifactor authentication, and workload security.

10. Keep your employees updated on security-wise

Invest in the education of your employees to keep them abreast of what is happening. Education is essential to enforce any far-reaching prevention measures in cybersecurity.

With the proper knowledge, users can detect spoofed messages and wade off smishing, CEO fraud, phishing, and vishing attacks. When users become fully aware of the risk of clicking a supposed harmless link and downloading a suspicious program, they will have to rethink before doing it.

It will be a win-win for both users and the company as it will save stress and help the company save money it would instead use for any Ransomware.

UNDERSTANDING THREATS AND VULNERABILITIES

To effectively contain any cybersecurity threat, you must understand these threats and see how vulnerable you are to succumbing. These are some common cyber threats that could undermine your cybersecurity security:

1. Malware

Malware is short for malicious software, and it includes any executable code or program created to purposefully cause havoc in a network, server, or Computer. Malware is a well-known type of cyber attack, and this is so because it branches into many subsets like trojans, viruses, keyloggers, crypto-jacking, worms, spyware, Ransomware, and any other kind of malware attacks that make use of software maliciously.

2. Phishing

Phishing is another cybersecurity threat that can harm vulnerable networks or systems when successful. In phishing, SMS, calls, emails, social media, phone, and social engineering are the standard techniques employed to lure unsuspecting individuals into sharing sensitive information such as account numbers and passwords or make them download malicious files that can introduce viruses into their network when installed whether in their phone or Computer.

3. Denial-of-Services (DOS) Attacks

This form of cybersecurity threat uses the technique of flooding, where it bombards a network with false requests to disrupt business activity. In this attack, users are denied access to their routine tasks like accessing websites, emails, their online accounts, and other resources within the compromised network or Computer. Although DOS attacks may not result in data loss, systems can be restored without ransom. However, they can cost the affected organization significant money and time to restore business operations. We are missing out on another: the Distributed Denial of Service (DDoS), which differs from DoS in the origin of attacks. While DoS attacks come from a single system, DDoS attacks originate from multiple systems. Also, DDoS attacks are more challenging than DoS attacks due to the number of systems involved, which would take time to identify and neutralize to halt the attack.

4. Identify-based Attacks

According to the reports, 80% of breaches use compromised identities and take approximately 250 days to identify. The sad part of this attack is that it is complicated to detect. It occurs when a user's credentials are compromised, and the adversary is pretending to be the user. It makes it all the more difficult to tell a hacker from a real user using standard security measures or tools.

5. Spoofing

This is a technique often used by cybercriminals. These cybercriminals disguise themselves and pretend to be known or trusted sources. This way, adversaries can engage with the target and gain access to the systems or devices to install malware, extort money, steal information, or even install harmful software onto their devices.

6. IoT-based attacks

When IoT-based attacks are mentioned, I am referring to cyberattacks that target the Internet of Things (IoT), network, or device. When a network or device is compromised, the hacker can have control of the device, steal valuable data assets, or even join a group of infected devices to develop a botnet, which the attacker uses to launch DoS or DDoS attacks.

7. DNS Tunneling

This cyberattack depends on domain name system (DNS) queries and feedback to move past the standard security protocols while transmitting data and code within the network. Once a hacker successfully gains entry, they can thoroughly take charge of the command-and-control activities. This tunnel allows the hacker to find a route to finally lose malware or even choose to extract data, sensitive information, or IP by carefully encoding it into DNS responses.

There has been a spike in tunneling attacks recently due to the simplicity of their deployment. There are even free and accessible tunneling tool kits online.

8. Insider threats

Insider threats are actors from within the organization that act in ways that not only compromise the organization's cybersecurity but also endanger their operations for their benefit. They could be former employees or current staff with direct access to the organization's network, intellectual property, sensitive business data, and knowledge of the business process, company information, and other vital information needed to initiate the attack. Although not all insider threat actors may be malicious, some may be acting out of negligence, and to deal with this, the organization has to implement a comprehensive cybersecurity training program to teach stakeholders to beware of any potential attack, including those from an insider.

9. Supply Chain Attacks

This cyberattack is aimed at trusted third-party vendors that offer needed software to the supply chain. The software supply chain attack begins with an injection of malicious code into an application to infect all users of an app. On the other hand, hardware supply chain attacks involve the physical parts for the same purpose. A software supply chain is especially vulnerable because most modern software is not written from scratch and involves different components from third-party to open-source code and propriety code from vendors.

10. Code Injection attack

This attack involves attacking malicious code into a vulnerable network or computer to change its operability.

HOW TO RECOGNIZE POTENTIAL VULNERABILITY

Sharing too much personal or business information online: Hackers carefully and patiently collect every bit of information from your socials to reach a satisfactory level where it becomes helpful, and they can do much harm with it. Sharing too much of your personal or business information online opens you up and makes you vulnerable to hacker exploits.

It would be best to be more active about passwords: entering passwords each time you want to open an app and sign in to an account can be tiring. With an additional layer of security, using multifactor authentication can make one lazier to keep up. Being lazy to keep up will make you more vulnerable to cyberattacks.

Casually using public wifi: having public wifi allows you access anywhere. It will enable you to connect and do your work seamlessly. But the not-so-good part about public wifi is that it has many security loopholes that can be exploited, which could make you vulnerable too.

Having too many unvetted apps: apps on our devices assume a significant part of our device usability. But apps are notoriously risky in terms of security and privacy. Having too many of them in your devices and vetting them can make you vulnerable to cyberattacks.

Becoming too comfortable online: When you become too comfortable online, you can easily let out things that are supposed to be private, and it also gives hackers much time to stalk you. This way, they can exploit your carefree nature, and you will become vulnerable to their attacks.

Lack of a unified family security strategy: With every family member owning multiple devices, a broad security gap can only be closed with a harmonious family security strategy. Otherwise, devices may be compromised, making other family members vulnerable.

Ignoring updates: Now and then, software vendors release updates to improve the security of their software or devices. If, for any reason, you ignore these updates, then you may be setting your devices or network for compromise.

Case Study

A typical example of Ransomware is the WannaCry attack that affected thousands of computers globally. The attackers exploited the network by encrypting data and demanding Bitcoin in payment to unlock files. This attack could have a devastating consequence that can leave businesses crippled and unable to get back on their feet. It impacted the healthcare organization so much that there were delays in medical procedures and compromised patient care.

KEY CYBERSECURITY CONCEPT

Encryption

Encryption is passing a message in a coded form that prevents unauthorized access to read or understand its content. Encryption is like sending a letter to a friend, and you don't want the mailer or anyone to be able to read it. Knowing they can easily break the seal and read the latter, I can choose to convert every word into code that my friend can understand. So, this means no one can see what the latter entails because they are unreadable. But once it gets to my friend, he knows what every code in that letter means, and he can convert it into readable text and understand the content. What I just did was encrypt a letter. The same analogy goes for data encryption in the network. Encryption prevents malicious hackers from accessing the information embedded in data.

CIA

Confidentiality: this is a process by which organizations protect data from unauthorized access. It keeps sensitive information safe and secure, which can improve customer trust.

Integrity: It entails maintaining complete and accurate information and protecting it from being altered.

Availability: This is where data accessibility to authorized viewers is discussed, and those given authority here can make changes if they choose.

Cyberattacks: Understanding what cyberattack means can help you set up effective preventive measures to contain potential threats. Some common types of cyberattacks include.

Malware: This is a type of software designed to disrupt network systems. They can bypass any authorization requirements, expose information, or deny authorized access to gain entry.

Phishing: phishing is a technique used by attackers to get login details through spam emails and false information.

Advanced Persistent Threat Persistent: These are sophisticated and prolonged attacks using phishing, social engineering techniques, or malware.

Software patches: These are security lapses or vulnerabilities in software that allow hackers the opportunity to attack a network.

SECURING THE CLOUDS AND APPLICATIONS

In our digital world today, data floats in the cloud, meaning anyone can have access. That is why you must know how to secure your data in the cloud. But before getting ahead of ourselves, what exactly does 'Securing the Cloud' mean?

EXPLORING CLOUD SECURITY FUNDAMENTALS

To get a clearer picture of what we are talking about, imagine placing your valuable item outside like a diamond where everyone can see it and then walking back home unbothered. You know it is unsafe and could go missing because it is valuable. You must secure it in a safe and keep it in a place where only you or anyone you choose to see it. Now, that is what securing the cloud means. It simply puts your valuable item (data) away from public access. It is just like putting your most treasured items in a vault. But other things besides the cloud need security. How about the applications that allow you to access this cloud? They must also be secured to avoid compromising the cloud's security. If we must secure one, the same must be said for all to have a smooth functioning system.

Think of cloud security as bringing together procedures, security controls, policies, and technologies to secure your assets on the cloud. The assets vary, including applications, data, infrastructure, or services. Suppose you have come across 'cloud computing security.' In that case, you may know about cloud security because they are often used interchangeably.

In our cyber world today, an essential factor pushing the boundaries of digital transformation is embracing cloud computing at a speedy rate. It has become too important to ignore for both government and businesses that seek to foster collaboration and innovation. This trend became more common during COVID-19, which spurred the hybrid culture of remote working. However, to achieve any success, our cloud must be secured to bring about the transformation.

Cloud Security can help us manage many issues, from unauthorized access, misconfiguration, and lack of visibility to insecure interfaces/APIs, malware, distributed denial of service (DDoS), malicious invaders, etc. There must be a collaboration between various organs like cloud service providers, organizations, and users to secure the cloud successfully.

WHY CLOUD SECURITY IS DIFFERENT FROM TRADITIONAL DATA STORAGE

Cloud computing has many benefits, but security concerns are ones to pay attention to. Given its dynamic and evolving nature, many security threats have continued to try to undermine the benefits of cloud computing in recent years. Frequently, cloud security is mistaken for IT security, so knowing the differences would help you better understand why the word 'cloud,' as used in cybersecurity, can be said to be secure.

1. Going beyond traditional perimeter defenses: Accessibility is essential in security. The conventional environment can control the access of data and information using a perimeter security model and ensuring that the cloud environment is well connected. This allows the traffic to bypass traditional perimeter defenses. While it facilitates traffic, data and systems become vulnerable to threats from account hijacks, credentials management, malicious insiders, unsafe application programming interfaces, and poor identity. But to prevent unauthorized access to your cloud, you must use a data-centric approach. Here, more priority has to be given to data encryption, multi-factor authentication, authorization process, and throughput security.

2. Data Storage and Backup: Backups housed onsite or on several sites and redundancy are often associated with traditional data storage. That means you must go beyond the manual effort alongside a strict backup plan. You would need to buy additional storage hardware to manage the risks of having data on multiple sites, making traditional data storage expensive. The debate about having more control over backups and data storage concerning deployment within premises continues to be discussed among Organizations. However, the situation looks quite different due to more reliance on an on-premises approach to proximity and human responsibilities.

Cloud-based storage is free from all the issues of traditional data storage because it is automated and removes any need for reliance on the IT team, shielding it from any physical damage. Trusted cloud service providers have spread high-tech data centers that are highly secure to forestall any attempt to compromise data. Data storage and redundancy in the cloud bring about a shared responsibility.

3. The increasing reliance of organizations on cloud security: In a data-centric and information-centric world, cybersecurity is a significant concern for Organizations that seek to protect their business operations and critical assets. There is hardly an organization that does not rely on data to carry out daily operations, making it even more important to have an integrated system into an infrastructure. It is more cost-effective, scalable, and safe. However, traditional servers' data retrieval and storage must be updated and secure. That is the main reason for organizations worldwide that cloud infrastructure is becoming a popular choice to address the critical need for analysis, data transmission, and storage.

4. Reducing cybersecurity threat: Rather than investing in the latest hardware upgrades or relying solely on IT teams, organizations are looking to trusted cloud hosting partners for their cloud computing needs, which reduces the need to depend on traditional security. Data security in cloud computing is better improved with automated processes such as network scanning by AI and updated emails, which further solves the issues bedeviled by traditional security measures such as human errors, outdated equipment, and missed maintenance headlines.

However, there is no hundred percent guarantee that traditional or cloud security can be entirely shielded from the occurrences of data breaches. However, cloud security can be more trusted in managing threats with automation than conventional security. With the evolution of security threats at a faster pace, organizations must rely on more than manual security protocols. But with cloud security, the CPAs are done automatically with AI defense tools. It takes a chunk of the burden of the IT teams and allows them to keep their eyes on other valuable innovations and strategies.

BASIC CLOUD SECURITY MEASURES

Cloud security breaches happen for several reasons, and one of the most important reasons is that cloud providers often do not have enough security measures to provide adequate protection for customer data. Also, customers may need to be made aware of the importance of securing their data and, as such, may not correctly be cautious when in cyberspace. Lastly, hackers may take a particular interest in cloud systems, knowing that access to massive data assets is possible. A lack of adequate cybersecurity can affect cloud service providers and users significantly.

While the cloud offers organizations a scalable and flexible means to access and store data, not every data created is equal, and some are more highly sensitive than others. All these must be considered, and special attention must be given to cloud security. It would help if you analyzed to check data sensitivity and decide which cloud strategy to use.

As the sensitivity of your data goes up the scale, your security should be more robust. Also, your organization needs to look into how its cloud strategy evolves because the more sensitive your data is, the more likely it will be to change your security measures. Here are some basic security measures you should keep in mind

1. Opt for a private cloud: Private clouds have control over users who access the public cloud, making them safer due to their high level of security. Organizations can have a tab over their data with such control over private clouds. However, the cost of maintaining private clouds is high, which may discourage many organizations from owning one.

2. Use Encryption: Encrypting files is a good security measure to protect data from unauthorized access. It functions by converting data into code, and only those with the correct key can decode them to reveal the information in the encrypted data, which makes it more difficult for hackers to access.

3. Have security measures at every level: Implement adequate security measures at every level in your cloud environment, even within data levels and your network applications.

- *With a network security measure, you can prevent unauthorized access to your cloud system.*
- *Can prevent data breaches by implementing application security measures.*
- *Data security measures allow you to protect all sensitive information against being stolen or accessed.*

4. Understand the shared responsibility model and what is covered in security. Customers and their cloud security providers protect applications and data in a shared responsibility model. It is a cloud cybersecurity approach. The shared responsibility is that cloud service providers secure the infrastructure, and the customers are responsible for ensuring their applications and data. Both parties must come to an understanding of vital security decisions such as encryption. Therefore, this shared responsibility model allows service providers and their customers to take charge of protecting their data.

5. Monitor cloud activity: Your organization needs to monitor its cloud activity to be sure that only those authorized have access to data. Also, it would be best if you never relented and always be on the lookout for signs of suspicious activity, which could be unexpected data transfers or suspicious login attempts.

6. Have a data backup plan: A data backup plan is essential to every cloud security strategy. In case of any data loss, having a data backup will be a guarantee to recover them without the fear of hindering your operations. Several reasons could lead to data loss, which could happen in different forms, including hardware failure, human errors, and software glitches.

Data backup plans could be offline, local, or cloud backups. While cloud backup is done on the Internet, local backup is done on local storage like an external hard drive, and offline backup is another data backup without using the Internet. Always go for a data backup plan that suits your needs.

7. Access control and endpoint security: Access control is a security measure created to restrict access to data and other resources. This form of control can deny unauthorized individuals access to any sensitive data.

Endpoint security, on the other hand, is designated for protecting devices connected to a network. With endpoint security solutions, you can prevent data breaches by keeping them safe from viruses, malware, and other threats. These two vital parts of our cloud security can protect the applications and data from unauthorized access or hackers' theft.

8. Introduce an effective password strategy: An important thing that must always be taken seriously is to have a strong password. Having a hack-proof password would make it easier to guess. A strong password should be at least eight characters long with upper and lower case letters, numbers, and special symbols.

You need to make sure you have different passwords for different accounts. This is so that a compromised password for an account does not jeopardize the security of the other version. Also, change your password regularly; the frequency depends on the sensitive data you're protecting.

9. Invest in staff training to help them understand attacks: It is crucial to invest in staff training to help them identify and respond to attacks. There are various cyber-attacks, including malware, denial-of-service (DOS) attacks, and phishing emails. Your staff should be able to identify these attacks and know what to do if they encounter one. Also, they should be able to relate any suspicious activity to the IT team.

10. Carry out Pen Testing to identify gaps: Pen testing is simply penetration testing designed to check for system vulnerability. They can be used to identify weaknesses in an on-premises and cloud system. Identifying the holes that attackers could exploit brings about improved system security.

Hackers can exploit vulnerabilities within systems. They use automated tools to gain access to resources or data and cause havoc in the system. For improved security and avoidance of data breaches, organizations must perform penetration tests and simulate hacking to find any weaknesses.

STRATEGIES TO SECURE CLOUD ENVIRONMENT AND DATA

The most critical part of cloud security begins with understanding the components that form your cloud stack. The different layers, identity, load balancer, storage, services, and computing, create potential targets and represent areas inside the cloud environment you need to secure.

Let's say you live in a hood where people constantly break into homes. As an individual concern, you must take precautions against intruders breaking into your home. You can double the security around your home by fitting high-quality locks and changing keys to prevent intruders from breaking in through your door. Let's look at some strategies to secure the cloud environment and data.

- **It needs a secure password**

Always go for the longest passphrase or password permitted in the system. Or, you can use more complex passwords like those that contain symbols, numbers, and letters.

- **Use a multi-factor authentication (MFA) at all places**

Having a strong password is good, but more is needed. So it would help if you had multi-layer protection, and introducing a second-layer authentication adds an extra shield to the user's login.

- **Develop most minor privilege roles**

Allow users access to only a few accounts and systems that give them room to be productive. It reduces the damage from a mistake or in case an actor gains unauthorized access to a given account.

- **Inactive accounts should be disabled**

When an employee no longer works with your organization, restrict all access they may have to every system. Also, their keys should be deactivated immediately. Inactive accounts create room for vulnerability as they are not continuously monitored as active ones, making more endpoints for attacks. When attacks are going on on inactive accounts, it may take a while before they are realized, which may compromise the whole system's security.

- **Observe for suspicious user behavior or compromised credentials**

Always enable real-time monitoring that combines analytics and machine learning to find suspicious activity or compromised credentials.

- **Improve your operating system**

Let go of all unused programs that only increase the attack surface for the overall system. Seize every opportunity to stay updated on service patches and packs.

- **Constantly look out for misconfiguration and anomalies.**

Introduce automation tools that can help you detect changes within the network environment and check for abnormal behavior.

- **Allow secure login**

Give out secure shell (SSH) keys to users. This SSH can keep data assets well-guarded as users move across unsecured networks.

- **Use firewall rules both inbound and outbound.**

Create a well-defined rule on what, who, and how much can be sent, received, and accessed both in and outbound.

- **Although most organizations may feel lazy to set up outbound rules, for a fact that hackers may try to steal sensitive data and even intellectual property, so it is necessary to set outbound regulations that are clearly defined.**

Also, it is vital to create firewall rules around the application layer instead of the network or transport layer, that is, at the IP and port information. Such a practice would forestall any attacker from piggybacking off on open ports like the domain name system.

- **Use only images you trust**

Get your images from trusted sources or build them from scratch. Avoid using images from sources that can't be trusted.

- **Manage your data access.**

With identity and access management, policies, and control lists, you can centralize your control permission to the storage. Also, with a security policy you can, your organization can enable or deny permission to account users using specific parameters such as IP address, dates, or whether the request came from a secure socket layer(SSL) encrypted session.

- **Classify data**

Automate data classification to understand the type of data and where to store it. While all this is running, ensure your data classification policies match security policies. Any violation of these policies should be flagged or remediated automatically.

- **Encrypt**

Adopt data encryption for both transit and data at rest. However, it is essential to note that metadata are only sometimes encrypted. Therefore, organizations should not attempt to store their sensitive information in cloud storage metadata.

- **Allow logging and versioning**

Organizations can preserve, restore, and retrieve data with versioning, especially if anything goes wrong. When versioning is turned on, businesses can quickly restore data to a new version by detecting a threat or application that causes data losses due to failure.

However, access logs allow an audit trail in case something or someone gets into your system.

- **Enable MFA before deletion, or do not allow deletion at all.**

Your organization should assign roles in their cloud infrastructure that prevent users from deleting data. Most cloud storage solutions allow features that require MFA before deletion is activated for any version of stored data in the storage layer.

- **Make use of source control.**

Always use source control version, deployment instances, and access to build. Doing it would reduce the surface area of your codes and limit the attack potential across your network.

IMPORTANCE OF PERSONAL RESPONSIBILITY IN CLOUD SECURITY

In our current digital world, there are just too many threats everywhere, and it is essential to have a second look at our security. It is not enough to own a smart device, laptop, or phone; understanding the fundamental principles of cybersecurity would help you make the best use of it. Initially, cybersecurity rested only in the hands of professionals, but not anymore, as cybersecurity accountability now extends to individuals using these devices.

Institutions and organizations need to spell out guidelines and best practices as a second layer of defense. However, the first line of defense is that the end-users must be fully aware of the prevailing threats lurking in the market waiting for them. There is no need to argue on who should be responsible for what. Instead, the focus of both parties should shift to personal ownership and unrelenting vigilance. Government regulations and independent checks could serve as means to ensure that cybersecurity protocols are adhered to. Still, the people who form the digital ecosystem's building blocks are secure, making it all the more important to educate the people and make them more aware.

WORLD EXAMPLES OF CLOUD SECURITY BREACHES AND THEY COULD HAVE BEEN PREVENTED

1. Facebook suffered a data breach in 2019, where more than 530 million users' data, such as user names, email addresses, phone numbers, and locations, were leaked and posted on a public database. However, Facebook claimed to have identified the problem and fixed it quickly. This data breach on Facebook points to the need for networks

and a better monitoring system to detect attacks and rapidly remove vulnerabilities.

2. In 2021, a hacker claimed to have breached LinkedIn and had access to millions of users' data. He offered to sell these data for 500million. How did the hacker do it? He allegedly exploited an API user ld by LinkedIn, which he found vulnerable. This breach is an eye-opener and shows why it is imperative to secure our cloud configuration, implement strong password management, conduct regular security audits, and vet third-party vendors.

3. In 2022, there was another data breach, but this time FleBooker was attacked. As a digital scheduling platform with a massive amount of sensitive data under its watch, the platform suffered a data breach that led to the names, email addresses, and phone numbers of users exposed. The company and platform used the AWS S3 bucket to store users' data. Still, it failed to put any reasonable security measures in place. This breach points to the importance of implementing adequate security controls in securing stored data.

BASICS OF APPLICATION SECURITY IN SOFTWARE DEVELOPMENT

Before delving into the basics of application security, we must first establish what it is. So, what is application security? The answer is straightforward: application security is simply the security measures that you can take at the application levels, which are aimed at preventing code(s) or data from within the app from being compromised, hijacked, or stolen. Application security entails the security that could come up in the design and development stage. It also entailed systems and approaches to secure the app after they are released.

In application, security software and hardware coupled with other procedures may be involved in identifying threats or cutting down on the number of security Vulnerabilities. For instance, a router is a form of hardware application security; It prevents anyone on the Internet from viewing your computer's IP address. Still, a good level of security measures are built into the software at the application security. This firewall determines what activity should be prohibited or allowed. Procedures include application security routine, which involves protocols like regular testing.

SOME GUIDELINES FOR CHOOSING AND USING SECURED APPLICATIONS DAILY

1. Please do thorough research: before considering using an application, you need to do adequate research about the app and see what previous users have to say about it.
2. Think again before typing: think deeply if your order is sensitive. Now, how secure is the application if it is sensitive? Do you want to risk your sensitive data in an unsafe environment?
3. Install only apps you use: there is no use having dozens of apps on your device when you don't use them. They only occupy storage space and even increase your vulnerability. So, stick with the app that you use regularly.
4. Always read the app's privacy policy: you want to see how much an app would use your data to serve your needs. By carefully reading it, see if you agree with the app's policy.
5. Avoid free apps: Many free apps are products of hackers and have bugs. They have deliberately developed these apps to send malware into your system and compromise its security. It would help if you avoid them entirely.

PERSONAL SECURITY AUDIT

There are several steps to reduce fraud, malware, online scams, theft threats, identity, etc. It could be strengthening your passwords or dealing with email from an unknown sender.

It is estimated that over 15 million individuals fell victim to identity theft in 2021, and such theft has caused victims some loss of about $ 24 billion annually. That is why protecting your assets and information is more critical now than ever.

Now, let's see a cybersecurity checklist that would be helpful to you.

Protect your devices

1. Be sure your software, operating system, and browser are the current version. This is because the newer version has updated security features to confront new and common threats and protect the system against other vulnerabilities. So, updating this software as soon as it becomes available would help you better secure your devices against malware.
2. Use a trusted antivirus product on your laptop or PC. This helps to protect your device from malware and other existing threats.
3. Download applications from only trusted sources like Google Play Store and App Store Store. Avoid apps from third-party app stores. Also, you must be careful not to download apps that pop up and ask you to download if they contain malware.

Guard your account login and secure them

1. Avoid reusing passwords on different websites and applications because it would make your accounts vulnerable when hackers crack the password.
2. Incorporate a password manager into your security tools. It will help you create complex, unique, and lengthy passwords and encrypt and store them.
3. Allow or activate multi-factor authentication (MFA) when logging into the website, any website, or application that you always use for your financial transactions or one that has access to your data.

Think before you click or share

1. Look again before clicking or opening an unsolicited text message or email attachment. You may be installing malware on your device if you do so.
2. Spam unsolicited emails or delete them instead of clicking the unsubscribe button, as doing so would tell the scammer that your email is active and in use, which invites more target attacks. Also, the unsubscribe button, when hit, may release malicious content on your device.
3. Think again before sharing personally identifiable information (PII) over email or text, especially when you have not initiated contact.
4. Be cautious about the amount of information you let out on social media, and be sure to lock your privacy settings on your account. Fraudsters may exploit your information and use it against you or those you may know.
5. Give only as much permission as necessary to your applications. Note that granting permission to an application may allow your contact, photos, location, and

data to be available to the app owner, which can undermine your internet privacy.

Cloud security entails safeguarding infrastructure, data, and applications on the cloud with controls, policies, technologies, and procedures. With a surge in remote work culture, adopting cloud computing has become a front burner in our digital world. Some vital issues that cloud security addresses include unauthorized access, insecure interfaces, and misconfigurations. Unlike traditional security, cloud security could consist of secure access, a shared responsibility model, and encryption. There are various strategies to secure the cloud environment, some of which are least privileged roles, continuous monitoring, and multi-factor authentication. However, taking personal responsibility for maintaining a solid cybersecurity outlook is crucial, prompting the implementation of cybersecurity principles.

Real-world examples of data breaches like those of Linked and Facebook show that monitoring and securing configuration is necessary. Application security, essential to preventing data theft, is vital in its development and subsequent deployment. There are guidelines for choosing a secure application, including cautious usage, vetted software, and research.

This chapter points to implementing the basic security protocols, learning from experiences, conducting personal security audits, and adopting strategies. By the above steps, individuals can contribute on their part and in no small measure to a more secure digital environment.

After learning how to secure your data in clouds and applications, it is time to see how to control data access and the critical role of encryption in keeping a digital identity.

IDENTITY, ACCESS, AND ENCRYPTION

Assuming your house is your digital identity, how would you secure it? In this chapter, you will better understand our online world's virtual keys and locks, giving you the tools you need to safeguard your digital presence.

COMPREHENSIVE VIEW OF IDENTITY AND ACCESS MANAGEMENT (IAM)

Identity and access management (IAM) is a structure for business policies, technologies, and processes that allows for managing digital or electronic identities. An IAM structure helps IT managers control user access to critical data in an organization. Various systems can be used for IAM, such as privileged access management, multifactor authentication, two-factor authentication, and sign-on systems. With these technologies, you can safely store your profile data and identity as a data governance function to share only relevant data.

THE IMPORTANCE OF STRONG IAM STRATEGIES TO PREVENT UNAUTHORIZED ACCESS

- **Enhanced security through single sign-on**

The IAM can allow users to access every application they require with just a set of credentials. This way, the risk of losing passwords or the fear of password theft is reduced, which makes it easier for users to adhere to strong password policies. Also, single sign-on can decrease the number of help desk calls concerning requests on password requests.

- **Improved security through granular access control**

IAM aims to help us establish a unique identity for an individual or item in all devices, such as router servers, mobile phones, sensors, and controllers. When a digital identity is set up, it must be monitored and updated regularly throughout the user's entire cycle.

- **More compliance with data security regulations**

With IAM, organizations can meet the ever-growing rigorous compliance requirements, including the California Consumer Privacy Act (CCPA) and the General Data Protection Regulation (GDPR). IAM helps control access to data and ensures that only authorized users can view or modify it. It relieves organizations and businesses from the burden of huge fines that could result in a case of non-compliance.

- **Improved visibility through identity governance**

IAM permits control and allows for better visibility of those who access your data and systems, giving insight into what they are doing after accessing it. This is very important regarding security because you can identify any potential threat and initiate steps to bring it under control. Not only that, but it also gives a comprehensive audit trial on the activity of users, which again offers valuable data in the case of a security breach.

- **Enhances security through two-factor authentication**

With IAM, you can add an extra layer of protection to your systems, which improves security by using two-factor authentication. This type of authentication, as you must have known, requires that users give two pieces of evidence for their identity verification. The authentication may include a password and security token or attributes. Two-factor authentication makes it difficult for attackers to access the system and data quickly, even after they may have a user's credential without their notice.

TIPS FOR MANAGING DIGITAL IDENTITIES AND ACCESS CONTROLS

For Personal Use

1. Use a strong and unique password
2. Enable a two-factor authentication (2FA)
3. Review your accounts regularly
4. Backup your files and valuable data assets
5. Improve your digital footprint awareness

For Professional Use

1. Apply the principle of least privilege
2. Use role-based access control
3. Establish an access control policy
4. Invest in identity and access management
5. Perform regular audits and reporting
6. Secure administrative access
7. Grant temporary privilege
8. Implement multilayer access control
9. Enable multi-factor authentication

THE ROLE OF CRYPTOGRAPHY IN CYBERSECURITY

Have you wondered how messages go to and fro between empires that are hundreds of thousands of miles away, with a third party getting a snippet of it? As old as those times with the absence of the internet, messages are passed using cryptography, and the receiver of the letters has the keys for each cryptic, which, when put together, reveals the content of the message. This is how messages are hidden from the views of others who could get the news and try to act on them maliciously. The same goes for the role of cryptography in cybersecurity.

Cryptography is a technique to secure communication or information using codes that only the receiver can understand and process accordingly. By using cryptography, you can prevent unauthorized access to information. 'Crypt' from the word cryptography means to hide, while 'graphy' means to write. The techniques used in cryptography to protect information are mathematical concepts derived from a set of rules that are based on algorithms that are converted to messages such that they cannot be easily decoded. The algorithms are used in generating cryptographic keys, verifying to protect privacy, digital signing, guarding confidential transactions, and browsing the internet.

Features of Cryptography

The features of Cryptography are:

1. Pass the information confidentiality: Information is kept hidden and only made and seen by those for whom it is intended. No one can access it unless accessed by the one for whom it is intended.
2. Integrity: with integrity, the information stored remains as it is. It is not modified in storage or during transmission between the two ends. If there is an attempt to alter it, it is detected quickly.
3. Non-repudiation: A sender or creator of a piece of information cannot hold back his intention to later on.
4. Authentication: the identities and destination of the sender and receiver are confirmed.

ROLES OF ENCRYPTION IN PROTECTING DATA

We all know how mailed letters are received. Now, assuming the latter is sent to you unsealed, what would come to your mind? You would suspect it has been tempered. That is where Encryption comes on. The seal to the mail later encrypts it from being accessed. However, because the seal was broken with the possibility that someone might have tempered it, Encryption works much more robustly so that no unauthorized person can access it.

COMMON ENCRYPTION METHODS AND THEIR APPLICATIONS

1. AES

AES stands for (Advanced Encryption Standard) and is a standard algorithm trusted by the US government and many other organizations. Also, AES can be found in the Arcserve Unified Data Protection (UDP) software. One good side of it is that it is efficient in 128-bit form, and not only that, it uses keys in 192 and 256-bit form for massive Encryption purposes.

So far, AES has proven to be waterproof against all attacks, except for some brute-force attacks that try to reveal messages using combinations in the 128, 192, and 256-bit cipher.

2. Triple DES

The triple DES was introduced as a replacement for the original Data Encryption Standard (DES) algorithm. It became vulnerable because hackers eventually learned how to trounce it. At a point, Triple DES became a widely recommended and used industry standard. It uses three keys, each of which is 56 bits with a total key length of up to 168 bits. However, experts suggested that 112 bits in key strength are the most correct. Although Triple DES is slowly going out of fashion, it is been replaced by the Advanced Encryption Standard (AES).

3. RSA Security

This public-key encryption algorithm is a standard for encrypting data used over the internet. Also, it is one of several methods used in GPG and PGP programs. It is considered an asymmetric algorithm due to the pair of keys it uses. It comes with a public and private key that allows you to encrypt and decrypt a message; the good side of RSA Encryption is that it produces a considerable batch of mumbo jumbo that costs attackers massive person-hours and processing power to break.

4. Twofish

This symmetric technique has keys up to 256 bits in length in its algorithm. However, it needs only a single key as a symmetric technique. Good enough, Twofish is one of the fastest in its class and best for use in software and hardware environments.

5. Blowfish

This algorithm is also designed to replace DES. As a symmetric cipher, it splits messages into blocks of 69bit while it encrypts each of them. Blowfish is famous for its high speed and general effectiveness. You can find blowfish in software categories ranging from platforms like e-commerce for securing payments to password management tools used to secure passwords. Blowfish is if you're looking for a flexible encryption method.

BEST PRACTICES FOR AUTHENTICATION, AUTHORIZATION, AND DATA ENCRYPTION

1. Use password-based authentication: This authentication is knowledge-based and depends on a password or PIN and a username. It is a prevalent authentication method and relatively straightforward. Pretty everyone who logs on to a PC uses a password.

2. Enable two-factor authentication: To enable two-factor authentication, the user must provide at least one authentication factor other than a password. A multifactor authentication requires two or more elements. Any other aspect can be the user's authentication type or one-time password (OTP) sent to their message or email. The factor can also include an out-of-bound authentication that entails a second factor sent on a separate channel from the previous device to reduce man-in-the-middle attacks. This authentication reinforces your security account because it will frustrate attackers. After all, they need more than just credentials to access an account.

3. Use Biometric authentication: This form of authentication uses the uniqueness of each fingerprint, relying much less on an easily stolen secret to verify if users own a particular account as claimed. The essence of biometric identifiers makes it a tall task for hackers to use them in hacking accounts.

4. Enable Single sign-in: With a single sign-in, an employee can use a single set of credentials to access multiple applications or websites. In this case, a user has an account with an identity provider (IdP) who offers a trusted source for the application, a service provider. Passwords are not saved with the service provider. Instead, the identity provider communicates to the site or application using tokens or cookies that the user can be verified through it.

5. Use Token-based authentication: This form allows users to log into accounts using their physical devices, such as a security smart card or smartphone. Token-based authentication can be utilized as part of MFA or to provide access without a password. Users can verify their credentials once for a predetermined period to reduce the need to log in repeatedly.

6. Use certificate-based authentication: In this form of authentication, digital certificates from certificate authorities and public cryptography are used to identify the user(s). The curtain has a public key and identification information, while a virtual private key is already stored.

Difference between authentication and authorization

Authentication is the process in which users can be verified before accessing an account or system. But authorization is yet another process that verifies if they are the actual owners or have permission for the access they are about to have or have already.

Let's use a typical everyday example to clearly understand what we are trying to discuss in the preceding paragraph. Let's say you go through security in an airport; you will need to show your ID to verify your identity during authentication to show you're not falsifying identity. When you arrive at the gate, you must present your boarding pass to the flight attendant for authorization to board the flight and to allow you access to the plane. That is how authentication differs from authorization.

TIPS ON HOW TO ENCRYPT PERSONAL DATA AND THE IMPORTANCE OF USING ENCRYPTION IN VARIOUS ONLINE ACTIVITIES

Tips on how to encrypt personal data

- **Use Encryption Tools:** Many encryption software tools can help you encrypt your files containing sensitive information or databases. For devices like Android phones, they come along with built-in Encryption features.

- **Use a Virtual Private Network (VPN):** with a VPN, you can have your connection to the internet Encrypted, which protects you from being monitored or intercepted.
- **Encrypt sensitive data:** it doesn't matter where your data is stored or how difficult you think someone can reach them; it would be best to encrypt all sensitive data.
- Secure your devices: With encryption, you can secure them, be they a phone or PC.
- **Use secure communication tools:** Most communication tools, such as messaging apps and email, offer users end-to-end encryption to protect their messages from being looked into or read by anyone other than the receiver of the message.
- **Manage Encryption keys effectively:** your Encryption keys closely and make sure they are securely stored because when a person with mischievous intentions gets hold of them, they can decrypt your data and access the information.
- **Use HTTPS for online activities:** HTTP encrypts data between your browser and the website you're on and offers you a safe environment for your online activities.

DATA ENCRYPTION PLAN WORKSHEET:

1. Design and communicate a data encryption plan:

To have a successful deployment, you need to start with a well-nested collaboration across teams to develop a plan for going forward. Bring in all relevant executives to get their support because it will be necessary to help you secure a budget and move your plan from where it is.

Also, it is essential to call in team members and database administrators who deal with data systems, your network, storage, or data security in your data encryption plan. Having these stakeholders on your side would help minimize the impact on performance and critical timelines during data encryption implementation.

The next thing to do is build a consensus on how the encryption should align with your priorities and the goals of your business to help everyone understand and know what to expect. Have a look again at the teams and systems on the ground. If need be defined, introduce a new group and assign a leader. You also need to know that separation of duty is essential to proper encryption and its vital lifecycle management, and that needs to be well spelled out from the onset.

2. Identify high-value data for encryption prioritization.

It is necessary to build a holistic view of the kind of data you have, its sensitivity, and its location each time there is deployment on numerous data sources on the cloud and on-premises. This stage can be complex and time-consuming. However, with data identification and mapping processes, you will surely be on a path to success.

Understanding underlying policies and access control will be handy in helping you know in what way your encryption strategy should work with adjacent technologies and established routines. You wouldn't have to do much work if you had a data recovery and classification solution because it can be automated and well-categorized for encryption prioritization. First, you would want to protect your valuable enterprise assets due to their sensitive nature and for a quick win that can be leveraged and build a case around return on investment.

How you define your critical data depends on your industry or business. The 2020 Data Security Survey of the International Data Corporation states that most security professionals and IT consider business-critical information and sensitive, regulated data the most needed protection.

Business-critical information, such as trade secrets, business plans, and intellectual property, exposes or makes up an organization's competitive advantage. At the same time, Sensitive, regulated data includes employee and customer information like their personal identity, health records, and social security numbers. Encryption of sensitive and regulated data often forms a key provision for most regulations.

3. Explore encryption technique

Once you have successfully formulated your strategy and understand your organization's most critical data, figure out what encryption technique will be necessary to protect your enterprise data at rest and in transit. We can categorize data encryption as to what they are deployed in the technology stack. It consists of four levels where data encryption is fully implemented: file system, application, entire disk or media, and database.

In most companies, file encryption can have an improved approach because its board supports most use cases. Also, file encryption is easy to deploy and operate.

As the stack In data encryption is brought in, it will be complicated to implement. It will significantly impact performance, and you will have more data protection. The goal here is to strike a balanced approach.

It would be best to consider how you would manage your encryption key. According to experts, the best way is to let your business control every encryption key, including those used in cloud data encryption. This delegation of duty and storage can be enforced so that the encrypted data is far from its encryption keys unless one fully secures access.

4. Choose an encryption provider.

You should know by now which encryption providers exist in the market. It is time to choose the vendor that best serves your needs. However, when selecting a vendor, you need to be cautious of the criteria for each product's feature, its functionality, and the kind of relationship you want. Your interaction with the provider should continue after purchase. A solution provider with a diverse product and service can offer advice, provide integrated solutions, and support your business growth.

For the encryption products, be sure to choose a vendor offering policy management and a centralized key that helps improve operations around data encryption and critical lifecycle management that allows you to upgrade quickly and shortly.

5. Think beyond deployment.

As soon as a solution is implemented and active, you must constantly monitor it for any violations or outliers. Also, you must continue improving alignment with your business and strategic goals and keep an eye on business growth and shifts to adopt an encryption plan as necessary.

Have a plan for your organization to move more days to the cloud. Look to the developers, application owners, and end-users to find who is scaling the most influence on your company's operations.

You should know that a more robust encryption strategy must adapt to business needs. Therefore, you should develop an approach that changes in technology and requirements from essential stakeholders.

Having gained a better understanding of protecting your digital identity and encrypting sensitive data, it is time to hop into the unexpected. In the next chapter, we will see how to respond to cybersecurity incidents effectively to prepare you for any digital attacks or threats.

RESPONDING TO CYBERSECURITY INCIDENTS

You have been busy with your systems and suddenly realize a breach. What would be your reaction? It would be either of these two: you would act immediately to contain the damage it could do to the system and your data, or delay for any reason and see it lead to a more severe cybersecurity issue. In this chapter, you will learn the right actions to take when a cybersecurity incident like this happens.

DETAILED APPROACH TO INCIDENT RESPONSE AND MANAGEMENT

You would agree that every building should have a fire evacuation plan. No one ever wished to see a fire incident, but such a plan still has to be in place to be ready for any eventuality. That is, when there is a fire outbreak, irrespective of the source and anywhere around the building premises, there is a plan to effectively put it under control with little or no damage caused at all. Having an evacuation plan in case of a fire incident is cost-effective because it saves things from going wrong and allows operations to be smooth for extended periods.

Now, we can liken the fire evacuation plan to an incident response in cybersecurity. Take incident response as a strategic and organized approach that can help you detect and manage cyber attacks to minimize the damages that could result in costs and recovery time.

Incident response is a topic under incident management. Still, incident management covers an enterprise's holistic approach to dealing with cyber attacks that brings different stakeholders from the HR, legal, IT teams, and executives into its fold. Incident response is part and parcel of incident management involved in taking care of technical cybersecurity, including other considerations.

There are six phases of incident response, and they are:

1. Preparation: this is the phase where you're all set for any cybersecurity incident.
2. Identification: this phase is where you interpret the nature and degree of severity of an attack to give a tailored response
3. Containing the threat: this is where you have figured out how to deal with the nature of the threat.
4. Eradicating the threat: after identifying the danger and figuring out how to deal with it, it is time to delete the threat.
5. Recovery from the incident: at this point, the system slowly and steadily returns to how it was before the attack, back to normal.
6. Post-incident analysis: in this final phase, you recollect all that has happened and record them accordingly so that

they can serve as a reference and help prevent a recurrence, assess, and respond.

STEPS FOR PREPARING AND RESPONDING TO CYBERSECURITY INCIDENT

1. **Preparation:** Identify your vendors and employees who would take charge of any potential incident and help them get established in the incident response role. So that when any cyber attack shows up, each knows their responsibility as clearly defined from the start.
2. **Detection:** Install monitoring software to provide regular and general watch over your network. Clearly define minor and significant events with a measured escalation process.
3. **Containment:** pick out the infected system and analyze it to see what caused it.
4. **Recovery:** Remove all things that have resulted in the infection, whether by blocking malicious IP addresses, patching holes, changing passwords, or fixing the vulnerabilities. Afterward, you can put your network back into service while complying with regulatory requirements. At this point, it is also necessary to use measures that protect the reputation and image of your brand.
5. **Post-Incident review:** Talk with relevant stakeholders about what you have learned and, take necessary steps to fix the identified cybersecurity issues and ensure that such an incident never happens again.

TIPS ON INITIAL ACTION TO TAKE IMMEDIATELY AFTER DISCOVERING A BREACH

1. Contain the breach: the first thing to do immediately after discovering a violation is to contain it. This is so that you can stop it from further spreading, which will minimize the damage. Failing to include it timely enough could lead to massive losses beyond your imagination.

As soon as you make the discovery, alert the IT department or your security response team so that they can get to work immediately. During this process, they can locate the source of the breach, look for vulnerable points to secure, and even take things offline to prevent widespread outspread. Since most breaches are possible with insider's help, deliberately or not, you must restrict your employees' privileges over the user's account until you have better details.

While your team gets busy resolving the breach, record it, save a copy for yourself, and write down what is discovered and done. Lastly, avoid deleting any data because all you have recorded will be useful.

2. Assess the damage: immediately after succeeding in containing the breach, run a check to see what has been affected. Check it whole, not just where the breach was discovered, because you may think it is restricted to a place that is more extensive than it is.

Run a check on your system logs to see the files or system accessed at the time of the incident, and looking into the records you have recorded would go a long way to help you get to it. As you dig into finding out what accounts or data were affected, you also need to consider the damages it could do to the future of your business.

Learning to determine the degree to which your data was breached would give you an idea of what you should do next. Let's say you discovered that the attacker got hold of your employee's names or emails; you will be able to tell that phishing is a threat you may have to deal with in the future. After that, you can pass on the information to all within the organization, instruct them to stay alert, and introduce anti-phishing training to help them deal with phishing attacks better.

3. Inform all those affected: the next thing you want to do after assessing the damage done is inform all customers, employees, or partners that may have been affected during the incident. A good cybersecurity practice is constantly educating your staff to report suspicious activity and respond appropriately to all emergency cases. However, they need to be well informed about events to act accordingly. So, the faster the information gets around, the quicker it will be worked on to mitigate the impact.

Most regulations demand that businesses notify users of data breaches when they occur. Although there are no specific time-lines for such notification, the sooner you inform them, the better. According to the European General Data Protection (GDPR): "alert them without undue delay." Therefore, passing out the information a few days before it occurs should be the best way.

You should include what has happened and how it affected those involved when alerting them. Also, let them know what you're doing about it and how they can help by taking necessary actions, such as demanding that they change passwords, etc.

4. Test new security patches: While investigating the damage caused by the breach, your security and IT team should be able to patch up any vulnerability that may have led to the incident. Prompt and regular updates are essential throughout the processes. Still, it is equally necessary to ensure that your IT and security know how critical their job is, and once the problem is fixed, test-run it.

IT departments should always test security patches like a fire department tests fire hydrants against set standards to see if they can hold up in terms they are most needed. These tests are necessary to ensure that another attacker would not breach the network like the previous one. They provide the same test throughout the organization and are not restricted to where the incident occurred.

As your business grows, security systems and networks, as do the connectivity and complexities, become more interconnected. As a result, more attack surfaces are open and must be covered. That is why it is always brilliant to make penetration testing part of your business continuity plan. Whenever you make any changes to your IT environment, run a test through to see what kind of attack can cause a breach so that it doesn't suffer a similar fate when up and running.

5. Review and improve: consider this incident an opportunity to enhance your network and systems security outlook. After successfully fixing the Vulnerabilities, inform every stakeholder and deal with all legal issues. Then, call a meeting to review the situation.

Now, reflect on all that had happened, from how everyone responded and how those actions impacted the results. Answer these questions honestly: what worked well? And what didn't work well? The answer you arrive at can help you to improve your responses to any data breaches in the future.

With a well-structured business continuity plan, you can reduce the damages and costs of any future emergency. However, creating and refining such a plan demands a good understanding of the weaknesses and strengths within the systems and network.

IMPORTANCE OF COMMUNICATION DURING AN INCIDENT

Communication is crucial at a time of breach incidents for the following reasons:

1. **Risk management:** when communication is clear, stakeholders can understand the depth of the breach, assess their risks, and take necessary precautions.to protect their data assets and systems.
2. **Transparency and trust:** you can build trust among your customers, employees, and regulatory bodies with open and transparent communication even in challenging situations such as a breach incident.
3. **Compliance and legal obligations:** most jurisdictions have legal requirements concerning notification and reporting of a breach incident. Therefore, accurate and timely communication makes it easier for organizations to comply with their obligations and avoid unwarranted penalties.
4. **Mitigation and recovery:** With communication, you can coordinate reasonable response efforts that allow your team to deal with the breach as soon as it surfaces to reduce the damages that may occur and also recover time.
5. **Learning and improvement:** after the incident, communication can facilitate the evaluation and analysis of any response procedures, allowing Organizations to identify Vulnerabilities, make improvements, and tighten any loose ends in their cybersecurity outlook for the future.

6. **Reputation management:** how a business manages its cybersecurity can significantly impact its reputation. Therefore, be open and honest in your communication because it will control the reputational damage that could result while preserving your brand choice.

STEPS TO COMMUNICATE EFFECTIVELY WITH STAKEHOLDERS

1. Assess the situation: Before sending out messages, you must assess the situation to collect as much information as possible. Find out the nature, scope, and impact of the attack. If possible, get to know who is responsible and the motives behind the attack. Have an accurate estimation of time to restore operations to normal. Know the legal and regulatory implications. Understand the attack's risks and the opportunities for your organization. With all that, you will have a clearer picture, allowing you to draft a better communication strategy and objectives.

2. Identify your stakeholders: What you need to do next is identify who your stakeholders are and give priority to each according to the degree of influence they have on your business. Understand their needs, concerns, and expectations so you can tailor your messages accordingly. For instance, your customers may be eager to know how they are affected by the breach, and your employees, on the other hand, may want to learn how to deal with the attack and support the recovery process. Also, regulators would look to see how you complied with set standards and relevant laws during this incident.

3. Choose your channels: after identifying your stakeholders and their needs, it is time to choose a suitable channel to communicate your messages to them. Your channel depends on the situation, whether through phone calls, emails, press releases, live meetings, websites, webinars, or social media. Be sure to consider the advantages and disadvantages that each channel has that is, in terms of its speed, interactivity, reach, credibility, and cost. Coordinate your channels and be sure they are consistent and accurate throughout.

4. Deliver your messages: follow best practices when delivering your messages to communicate effectively during an attack. Be honest and transparent about the attack and what happened. Tell them what you're doing to fix it and what they should expect. Also, you need to be empathetic and address your stakeholders politely. Let them know you understand their frustrations and how they are feeling. Be timely and proactive with your updates and feedback. You must be precise and clear when communicating technical terms and put aside acronyms and jargon that may lead to confusion. Speak confidently and positively while expressing your capabilities and confidence to deal with the crisis in your message.

5. Monitor and evaluate: it doesn't stop after you have delivered your message. You must monitor and assess to see how effective your communication is. Collect and analyze feedback from stakeholders through their comments, compliments, complaints, and questions. Also, track and record the outcome of your communication by gauging its level of understanding, trust, awareness, loyalty, and satisfaction. Adjust you improve your communication tactics and strategies according to the feedback and outcomes you receive.

STEPS TO COMMUNICATE INTERNALLY DURING A CYBERSECURITY INCIDENT

1. Communicate your strategy on the cyber attack: your employees should know what exactly to do in a cyber attack incident, the procedures and actions to take, how to handle time-sensitive information, and the contact to make as quickly as possible. This is even more important for staff working remotely because they may not have the support of a tech team to answer most critical questions. Therefore, you need to have a cyber attack response plan in place and ready outlining the necessary steps each employee at every level of your organization must take in an attack. Effective communication serves as a tool for disseminating your strategy throughout the Organization. Also, internal communication platforms allow the flow of updates and information to give everyone clarity on what they should do.

2. Make cybersecurity a part of your corporate culture: for most organizations, cybersecurity is simply a list of dos and don't, like encrypting a file, not opening an email attachment, or hitting a link in the email from an unknown sender. However, such an approach to Cybersecurity isn't efficient when engaging employees and evaluating inventive ways hackers can launch an attack. For more effective cybersecurity, it needs to be part of a broader organizational culture, and one way to achieve this is by keeping employees up-to-date with cybersecurity by reinforcing the message throughout the Organization through internal communication. Much more than sending out tips and examples, you can leverage your internal communication platforms to create more engaging content such as pop-up quizzes, kudos to the employees who took steps to keep data safe, and storytelling.

3. Tailor your messages to various groups without your organization according to their roles: a crucial benefit that internal communication platforms bring is that they help direct your message to various and specific groups of employees, such as within certain departments, production sites, or regional offices. These groups from the different departments have their particular cybersecurity concerns. For instance, employees at the head office would not have a system vulnerability similar to those collecting sensitive data in the field. Having effective internal communication would help you focus your instructions and advice about cybersecurity in more engaging, meaningful, and relevant ways for each group of users

4. Organize training for your employees to keep them updated about recent Cybersecurity threats: Hackers are ever relentless and always coming up with new tricks and developing sophisticated means to steal information. Incorporating cybersecurity into your employee's training programs is essential, but you can't stop there. You must help keep employees updated about the latest trends and threats that they must watch out for through continuous training coupled with internal communication. Many platforms have features allowing you to conduct mock phishing exercises, demonstrate how new technology can be used safely, and share best practices.

5. Be organic: internal communication also helps provide a social network feel. Your employees should be able to publish and comment on posts, run quick polls, share videos, etc. These features can help promote cybersecurity in a more organic fashion such that it directly has everything to do with your employees' daily activity at work. Workers can share tips on a new piece of software, remind team leaders about a file that must not be sent out to a consultant, or share an article about a significant data breach. With a social network environment, employees can feel safe to ask questions and voice their concerns. Managers can also find it helpful in collecting ideas from staff who use business applications daily.

CASE STUDY OF EFFECTIVE INCIDENT RESPONSE

A phishing attack was targeted at Cloudflare in August 2022, and many of its employees and members of their families received phishing messages on their phones. These SMS received on their phones come with an official-looking type of domain that was only registered about 40 minutes before the phishing messages came in. Even though an authentication system is in place, and it requires a TOTP or time-based OTP, the attackers tried to beat that by setting up a real-time system to overcome the authentication mechanism.

Although Cloudflare was not directly affected by the breach, its employees and their families were the most affected by the phishing attack. The attackers could not succeed in breaching Cloudflare due to the FIDO2-compliant security key that Cloudflare used. These keys are designed in such a way that they are tied to users and implement origin binding, which the attackers find very difficult and impossible to beat.

After identifying the attack, Cloudflare blocked the phishing domain from its gateway and collaborated with domain providers to deregister it. It was further investigated to catch any other signs of compromise to reset such compromised credentials when identified so that they never become a source for the attackers again. For faster identification, Cloudflare updated its identification system to check such attacks in the future.

CLOUD SERVICE TEMPLATE: QUICK THINKING AND EFFECTIVE PLANNING

A go-to place for your quick and effective incident response solution is the cloud service providers: they have an incident response template that can counter any security threats in the cloud environment most of the time. The templates are designed to guide through procedures and tools relevant to a more effective response. These procedural steps include monitoring software to detect incidents, documentation for handling incidents, emphasizing rapid containment of threats, and activating plans to respond to attacks. Activating your plan according to what works for you is very important.

QUIZ:

1. Misuse and Misappropriation are a form of attack that results in _____.
2. For more effective cybersecurity, there is a need for effective communication. True/False
3. _____ is the first step to take after a breach incident.
4. Communication must be tailored to an individual or business's impact on your organization/company. True/False
5. An incident response plan is necessary to contain any breach incident. True/false.

Responding to cybersecurity incidents must begin long before an attack from an attacker to breach your network or system surfaces. This is so that you have more time to respond effectively, protecting the integrity of your system and your brand's reputation.

Now that you know how to respond to cyber incidents, let's delve into the broader picture of cybersecurity governance, compliance, and risk management, where prevention meets policy and planning.

GOVERNANCE, COMPLIANCE, AND RISK MANAGEMENT

Do you know that not complying with cybersecurity laws may cause you more troubles that could mess up things? Imagine yourself driving and ignorant about the traffic rules. In this chapter, I will guide you in understanding the traffic rules of the digital highway.

UNDERSTANDING SECURITY GOVERNANCE FRAMEWORK

Sports are often highly organized events, and there are rules to bring any events set out until their termination. The rules serve as the principle or framework for organizing activities concerning that sport. The same applies to a security governance framework. Security Governance Framework is or are the guiding principles upon which to append your cybersecurity.

We can say that information security governance is a framework of policies, strategies, and practices that allows your organization to align resources to protect its information using cybersecurity measures.

Also, you must know that governance policies are essential for your business organization due to ad hoc security protocols, which is hardly ever enough as IT infrastructure and modern cybersecurity threats evolve. So having information governance, centralized accountability and security, and planning in your organization would help you always to have various overlapping priorities well taken care of. The priorities are:

1. **Resources allocation:** this includes funding for training materials, executive positions, and technology concerning information security and compliance.
2. **Compliance:** Your organization must adhere to industry standards or operational framework according to its needs.
3. **Accountability:** your management hierarchy must be accountable for decision-making and process development.
4. **Implementation of advanced security measures:** to implement an advanced security measure, you need to understand risk management, be proactively preventive, and use tools such as AIs, penetration tests, or vulnerability scanners.

THE ROLE AND IMPORTANCE OF A FRAMEWORK IN SHAPING AN ORGANIZATION'S CYBERSECURITY STRATEGY

The role and Importance of a framework in Shaping an Organization's Cybersecurity strategy includes:

1. **Reduced risk:** your organization can effectively identify and mitigate cybersecurity risks when it adopts the cybersecurity framework, which reduces the potential for any successful cyberattack.
2. **Improved security posture:** Having a cybersecurity framework in place allows you a structured approach to managing cybersecurity risks, and in turn, it generally improves your organization's security outlook.
3. **Consistency:** with a cybersecurity framework, you consistently manage your cybersecurity risks throughout your organization and allow the various departments and employees to stick to a particular guideline and best practices.
4. **Compliance:** most cybersecurity frameworks have various regulatory requirements, making compliance more accessible for organizations and their industry-specific regulations.

POPULAR FRAMEWORK AND THEIR FUNDAMENTAL PRINCIPLES

Let's look into some popular cybersecurity framework and their principles. The framework comprises six core components that can help you nurture and develop maturity in your security Governance program.

1. Understand your organizational context: you can't build any governance strategy without understanding your organization's direction. From a security standpoint, it would be best to look closely at your organization's primary business practices, geographical footprint, product portfolio, culture, ethos, and customers. It will allow you to have answers to essential questions that bother you, such as who does what, from whom, and why they do it. Press further to understand the structure you would prefer for your organization, and check out current security standards, frameworks, guidelines, and regulations.

2. Understand how information security functions operate: you need to understand better how security functions operate. Have a general review of existing security policies and see if they are very effective. Also, you need to figure out the current state of security procedures, tests, activities, exercises, and projects and the level of control you have over your information security with a clear roadmap to achieve your purpose. Acquire the capabilities and skills of security practitioners and know how their responsibilities. Now, use that to set a benchmark for your industry's best practices to help you reveal the loopholes in your activities and capabilities.

3. Plot your information security governance framework: There must be highlights in the government documents in high-level language aimed at governance programs in connection with business risk. In this document, there must be a clear outline of the steps to take to fulfill your security goals with clearly defined roles and responsibilities of the security function. Not only that, but it should also outline the support it is most likely to extend to the executives, teams, and board members. With it, you should be able to communicate what information security will do, the kind of culture you are trying to build, and what way you will choose to achieve it.

4. Put the outlined strategy to work and have your controls: after securing your governance strategy, develop a comprehensive list of standards, methods, procedures, and policies to achieve your information security strategy. Ensure that your employees are accountable and let them know what you expect from all within the organization and the responsibilities the information security will address. Your policies should take care of what businesses must do to shield themselves and write out steps to tackle incident response and reduce its effect if there is a cyber attack or a breach.

5. Gain the support of senior management: you need the support of members of the board and executives to implement a practical governance framework. Security teams could be on a fruitless venture if they have no backing from the members of boards and top executives, which means their efforts would go unnoticed, having little or no impact on the organization and its culture. Governance demands active leadership that takes charge of things head-on and can force out the benefits for the overall good of all. There, you need to have a steering committee or forum that brings together senior management executives and individuals from the IT, legal, marketing, operations, procurement, data protection, and other relevant stakeholders.

6. Create awareness to influence behavior: create an elaborate and continuous training program that contains safer ways of working throughout the organization. This way, the number of complaints reaching the security team desk will be significantly reduced, which allows more time to identify the gaps in the existing government program. The more people realize the benefits of security governance, the greater the appreciation and influence it will have on the organization's security culture.

COMPLIANCE WITH CYBERSECURITY LAWS AND REGULATIONS

There are many benefits to derive when complying with cybersecurity laws and regulations. But if you choose to ignore them, you may be setting yourself and the reputation of your business up for legal consequences. Every industry has laws and regulations guiding it, so cybersecurity is no exception. Let's say a food industry, for instance, fails to abide by specific rules concerning the safety of its products, and a customer becomes affected as a result. Suppose it happens that the trace of the harm goes back to the industry. In that case, the food regulation industry will penalize that industry, and the customer may demand compensation for any damages caused. Such an industry may face severe lawsuits that would drain it financially and damage its reputation.

The same goes for compliance with cybersecurity laws and regulations. Now let's look at some of the importance of complaints.

1. It protects you against fines and other costs: compliance with cybersecurity laws and regulations keeps you safe from becoming a scapegoat for regulatory bodies. It keeps more money in the organization's purse that can be used to execute other projects. But if otherwise, that money may go into paying fines or compensation for damages caused due to non-compliance issues. These are most likely the consequences that you will be facing if you refuse to comply with laid down rules and regulations:

- HIPAA: You would pay about $ 50,000 for each default, depending on the level of culpability you found yourself.
- GDPR (EU): you may risk paying 20 million euros as a fine for violation. Twenty million euros is about 4% of global annual revenue. Now, that gives you an idea of what may be waiting if you fail to comply.

- California Consumer Privacy Act (CCPA): you may risk $2,500 to $7,500 for each violation.

2. Build trust and brand reputation: complying with cybersecurity laws and regulations keeps you in the excellent book of customers. The customers feel safe having their data in your system, and that's because of the trust and confidence they have towards your business. It will even help in terms of trouble. In case of a breach, customers would still invest their trust in you, knowing that you can secure their data. This will improve your reputation and attract more patronage.

3. Shut down risk: hackers always look for weak spots to exploit, and that is how they can gain entry to access your data files. This is only possible when you're off guard. But complying with cybersecurity laws and regulations keeps you on your toes to be watchful. It allows you to quickly counter threats by deploying your security procedures and configuration to reduce attack vectors, blocking all vulnerable points.

4. Access control and accountability support: accessing data is a crucial vulnerability. So, allowing only those who need the data for their job to access it will reduce the risk of breach incidents by tightening loose ends. Having access control is an effective IT security compliance strategy. This allows only vetted individuals to access the data there, keeping hackers out.

5. Encourages operational benefits: complying with cybersecurity laws and regulations is a recipe for better business performance. It mitigates the impact of a breach incident and positions your business at a competitive advantage against your competitors.

CYBERSECURITY LAWS AND REGULATIONS

The following are cybersecurity laws and regulations that you should know:

- **Cybercrime:** although it depends on the jurisdiction and what constitutes an administrative criminal offense. However, cybercrime constitutes hacking and denial of service attack, infection of systems with malware, phishing, offering or sales of hardware, identity theft, unsolicited penetration testing, or any other activities that threaten the integrity or confidentiality of any system, network, or device.
- **Cybersecurity laws:** these are laws that help in the detection, mitigation, prevention, monitoring, and Management of breach incidents. They include trade secret protection laws, confidentiality laws, data breach notification laws, e-privacy laws, data protection laws, and so on.
- **Preventing attacks:** Does your organization have permission to use beacons, honeypots, and sinkholes to protect itself against breaches?
- **Specific sectors:** you must find out too if legal requirements or market practices concerning information security vary across various sectors of businesses within your jurisdiction.
- **Corporate governance:** how would a failure by your organization cost it in preventing, mitigating, managing, or responding to a threat?
- **Litigation:** this concerns any private or civil action that may come up concerning a breach incident or element regarding an action that would be required to be fulfilled.

- **Insurance:** you need to find out here if your organization can have insurance against cybersecurity incidents within your industry.

TIPS TO STAY UPDATED WITH CHANGING LAWS AND REGULATIONS

Keying into new regulatory changes can be challenging for MSPs, especially if you're new. However, several simple steps must be taken to adapt to these new regulations.

The first thing you need to do as an MSP is to adopt and keep to cybersecurity standards or framework to key and support your primary industry. The NIST cybersecurity framework or CIS controls are an excellent starting point for most MSPs.

After that, continuous security awareness training, change management, inventory management, and constant vulnerability assessments are essential to successfully implementing the security program.

Lastly, as an MSP, you must establish a clean and easy Incident response plan and ensure you regularly test with employees using the tabletop exercise.

TECHNIQUES FOR MANAGING CYBERSECURITY RISKS

You will agree that health insurance has tremendously helped improve healthcare delivery to people every day and, as a result, the lifespan of individuals. Similarly, a cybersecurity risks management person is a health insurance company that has to deal with the health of our cyber systems and network, which affects humans' general health in many ways.

With cyber-risk management, organizations can understand the relationship between potential threats and their IT infrastructure. By understanding your IT infrastructure through managing Vulnerabilities, Organizations can better understand the complex interaction between cyber threats, security measures, and the cost of a successful attack from the threats.

IMPORTANCE OF RISK MANAGEMENT IN CYBERSECURITY

Some of the most important reasons why you should implement a cyber risk management strategy include:

1. **Prevention of attacks and mitigating the effects of a cyber attack:** you can identify threats to your organization when implementing a cyber-risk management plan. Risk management is like putting the proper defenses in place, which will help reduce the threats from any potential cyber attack.
2. **Reduces the costs of countering the effects of cyber attacks:** financial rewards are often the motivation behind most cyber attacks. Therefore, developing a cyber risk plan that can help you mitigate losses is necessary. Also, complying with laid down regulations in your industry would save your costs from fines and other non-compliant penalties.
3. **Improves the reputation of your business:** when you demonstrate your resolve to protect customers' data and take your overall cybersecurity seriously, it attracts the trust of your clients and customers. When you have their trust, you will surely enjoy customer loyalty- repeat patronage over a long period. This will give you a better competitive advantage against your rivals.

RISK ASSESSMENT METHODOLOGIES AND THEIR APPLICATIONS

Before discussing the methodologies and their applications, let's first understand what risk assessment is about; it is how organizations decide what they should do in the complex security landscape we find ourselves in today. Some vulnerabilities and threats follow you everywhere you turn. These threats could be external or internal or result from a careless user. Sometimes, the threats are even built from within the network itself.

Therefore, decision-makers must understand the cost and urgency behind other organization's risks and efforts to mitigate them. With risk assessment, one can set priorities and evaluate the probability of each risk and its potential impact. It is now up to the decision-makers to evaluate a mitigating effort that is most appropriate and prioritize according to the organization, timelines, and strategy.

THE METHODOLOGIES

There are several approaches that Organizations can take to assess their risks. However, each can help evaluate an organization's security risk posture. These methodologies are:

1. Quantitative: this method allows analytical strength to the process. Assets and risks attract dollars, and then the outcome of the risk assessments is presented in financial statements that the board members and executives can break down quickly. Decision makers often prioritize mitigation efforts due to their cost-benefit analyses.

Although a quantitative methodology may not be suitable, the risks or a couple of assets cannot be easily quantifiable. Compelling them to align in a numerical approach to judgment calls undermines the objectivity of the assessments.

Quantitative methods are not very straightforward, and communicating their results outside the boardroom may bring some confusion. Also, not every organization has the expertise that a quantitative risk assessment may require. That means other organizations would have to hire consultants to help with the financial and technical skills needed.

2. Qualitative: unlike quantitative, the qualitative methodology assumes a more scientific approach to risk assessment, like some form of journalistic approach. The assessors go about meeting people from all departments within an organization, and the employees there share whether or how they would do their job in case of any system eventuality that takes them offline. The assessors then use this information collected to categorize risks based on low, medium, or high.

With a qualitative risk assessment, we can have an overall picture of how risks can impact the operation of an organization.

Those within the organization will most likely better understand a qualitative risk assessment. While these approaches are usually subjective, the assessment team needs to develop more straightforward approaches, conduct interviews, ask unbiased questions, and interpret the results accordingly.

However, lacking a good financial background for mitigation options and prioritization of cost-benefit analysis can become difficult.

3. Semi-Quantitative: some organizations would instead go with combined methods to create what we call a Semi-Quantitative risk assessment. Using this approach, organizations can use a scale of numerical value from 1-10 or 1-100 in assigning numerical risk value. While risk items that hit the lower third are classed low risk, those in the middle and higher third are classed medium and high risk, respectively.

Combining qualitative and quantitative methodologies erases the need for critical probability and asset value calculations on a former and still gives more of an analytical assessment than the recent one. Therefore, semi-quantitative methodologies can bring more objectivity with a sound prioritization risk item base.

4. Asset-based: Organizations often choose an asset-based approach when assessing their IT risk. Assets comprise the software, networks, and hardware that allow an organization to handle its information. There are four steps in an asset-based assessment, and they are:

- taking inventory of all assets
- Evaluation to see the effectiveness of current controls.
- Identifying threats and Vulnerabilities of each asset.
- Assessing to understand each risk's potential impact.

Asset-based approaches are common due to their ease of alignment with the structures in IT departments, culture, and operations, and it is also easy to understand firewall risks and control.

The downside of asset-based risk is that it can't produce a complete risk assessment. Though we can't associate every risk with the information infrastructure, processes, software factors, and policies can make an organization vulnerable to an unpatched security firewall.

5. Vulnerability-based: this methodology broadens the scope of what we have come to understand as risk assessment and even beyond an organization's asset. It begins the process by examining the deficiencies and weaknesses within the system's environment.

After that, assessors come to identify the possibility of a threat that could find these Vulnerabilities alongside the attendant consequences.

Attaching vulnerability-based risk assessment to an organization's vulnerability management practices shows an effective vulnerability and risk management process.

Even though this methodology shows more risks than a strictly asset-based assessment, it is based upon well-known Vulnerabilities, which may not capture the full scope of an organization's threat.

6. Threat-based: this methodology allows for a more complete supply and assessment of an organization's general risk outlook. This approach considers the risk condition that brought it in the first place. Auditing assets will be part of the assessment because assets and their controls add significantly to these conditions.

When talking about threat-based approaches, we often look beyond the physicality of the infrastructure.

For instance, by carefully analyzing threat actors' techniques, assessments may reconsider mitigation options. Introducing cybersecurity training would help control attacks that may result from social engineering attacks. However, an asset-based assessment would instead prioritize some form of systemic control over employee training. However, a threat-based asset would always see the benefits of cybersecurity training in risk reduction at lower costs.

CREATING A RISK MANAGEMENT PLAN

- **Identify:** you need to determine every relevant asset of a technology infrastructure. Next, diagnose the sensitive data created, stored, or transmitted through these assets. Now, create a risk profile for each of them.
- **Assessment:** this is where your administrative acumen becomes most needed. So, you should adopt a trusted and tested approach to assessing and identifying security risks for critical assets. Having carefully evaluated and assessed it, decide how to efficiently and effectively allot time and resources to mitigate risks. The assessment methodology must allow you to analyze the relationship between threats, assets, vulnerabilities, and mitigation controls.
- **Mitigation:** have a clear definition of what your mitigation approach should be and strengthen your security controls for each risk factor.
- **Prevention:** Now, you must implement the processes and tools to help minimize your vulnerabilities and threats to your firm's resources.

Having covered the rules and strategies for securing our digital world, let's now turn to the rapidly evolving realm of interconnected devices. Next, we explore the unique challenges and solutions in securing the Internet of Things (IoT), a critical component of our digital ecosystem.

SECURING THE INTERNET OF THINGS (IOT)

In today's world, where everything has gone smart, from home thermostats to refrigerators and watches, to give us an improved lifestyle, all these are part of the Internet of Things. While we enjoy the benefits of these appliances and accessories, they could be a gateway for cybersecurity threats, and we shall be looking into how to prevent these attacks in this chapter.

CHALLENGES AND SOLUTIONS IN IOT SECURITY

Several challenges can be associated with IoT. But the good thing is that there are solutions to help you overcome these challenges. The Internet is open to all, but your data remains your identity on the Internet to browse. Imagine having a house filled with treasures.

Some of these challenges and Solutions in IoT Security include:

1. Poor secured network service: our devices use network services to access information, and that means your confidentiality, integrity, and authenticity can be compromised or even a possibility for unauthorized control over your devices

Hackers are relentlessly looking for ways to access your devices by finding communication services and protocol weaknesses. They do this to compromise your devices and access sensitive information between your device and the server. A standard attack type, man-in-the-middle (MITM) attacks, seeks to take advantage of these Vulnerabilities to get hold of credentials that can be used for endpoint authentication and rely on the same credentials to launch a more comprehensive scope attack. Therefore, securing our IoT communication using industry best practices is very important.

2. Guessable, weak, or hardcoded passwords: using guessable, invalid, or hardcoded passwords makes your IoT devices vulnerable to attacks. Through these means, attackers can launch other botnets and other malware. Safe password management in a distributed IoT ecosystem can be tedious and time-consuming, given that your IoT devices are managed over the Internet.

3. Lack of a secure update mechanism: updates are often released for devices. Updates are important because they have the latest security features to keep devices safer. But the downside is that there is hardly a secure update mechanism, a lack of a fast delivery (un-encrypted in transit), a lack of firmware validation on the device, a lack of notification of security changes due to updates, and a lack of anti-rollback mechanisms.

When software and firmware updates go without authorization, they could pose a big issue. They may be a significant threat in launching attacks against IoT devices, making them vulnerable to opportunistic attacks. The energy and healthcare sectors are especially vulnerable. Suppose you must secure software and firmware updates. In that case, you need more secure access to the verification source and know the update's trustworthiness.

4. Insecure ecosystem interfaces: backend API, mobile interfaces, and insecure web with the ecosystem and outside our devices could be compromised, including related components. This may arise due to insufficient input or output filtering, weak encryption, or even authorization or authentication.

It would be best to install a strong authorization and authentication mechanism. However, various other solutions are out there to secure the identity of IoT devices. Therefore, using an effective device identity mechanism each time a server and an IoT device communicate, the server can identify and separate rogue endpoints from valid ones through compulsory endpoint self-authentication.

5. Lack of device management: frequently, there needs to be more security support on devices used in production, such as update management, system monitoring, secure decommissioning, response capabilities, and asset management.

A severe security challenge primarily encountered in the IoT ecosystem is managing all devices through their lifecycle. When unauthorized devices gain access to the IoT ecosystem, they look through the corporate networks and intercept communication and traffic. The primary interest of IoT device management is the updating, operation, and provisioning of devices.

6. Using outdated or insecure components: insecure or deprecated software components and associated libraries could compromise devices. The issues with such components include using third-party software or hardware components from a compromised supply chain and the insecure customization of operating system platforms.

The vulnerabilities in software legacy systems or dependencies may compromise the security of the IoT ecosystem. The fact that manufacturers use open-source components to develop IoT devices creates a complex supply chain network that poses difficulty in tracking. Such components often come with various vulnerabilities, which users of the devices designed with this component are unaware of, creating an open threat landscape for possible exploitation.

7. Inadequate privacy protection: Most IoT devices retrieve data that should be well protected and processed to comply with existing privacy regulations like the CCPA or GDPR. Personal data can be medical information data used to drive behavior and consumption. Without appropriate controls, your user's privacy will be jeopardized with attendant legal consequences.

HOW TO MITIGATE THESE VULNERABILITIES

Manufacturers must install proper password management and authentication controls, making guessing and securing passwords quickly tricky.

Introducing a more secure network protocol like Transport Layer Security(TLS) and consistently updating your network services helps reduce vulnerability.

- Patching APIs regularly and introducing strict access controls to manage access to sensitive APIs and interfaces can be used to mitigate Vulnerabilities. Not only that, but implementing a secure communication channel between various components of the IoT ecosystem and using encryption can also help you reduce vulnerabilities.
- Implementing features like anti-rollback mechanisms, firmware validation, secure delivery (encryption), and digital signature on your devices allows manufacturers to address these Vulnerabilities more effectively.
- A regular update and patching of software and all components that are used in IoT devices (such as frameworks, libraries, and firmware), and developing a procedure to monitor and receive updates about security Vulnerabilities in components that are used for the IoT and it's ecosystem are excellent practices that can help to reduce exposure to attacks.
- Implementing the principle of privacy-by-design, applying encryption to secure sensitive data in transmission and storage, and obtaining user consent in collections and data usage are other effective mitigation methods.
- Using secure protocols such as HTTP and encryption techniques when transferring sensitive data, introducing a robust access control mechanism, and auditing data storage are effective practices to secure data when transmitting and storing data in IoT devices.
- Implementing effective authentication mechanisms such as enforcing access control to reduce device management functionalities and assigning unique device credentials to only authorized personnel can increase your attack risk.
- Another way to mitigate your Vulnerabilities is to change default usernames, configurations, and passwords in the

initial device setup and turn off all services and ports that are not needed to reduce your device's attack surface.
- Measures such as isolating or disabling debug ports, using a tamper detection mechanism, avoiding storing sensitive data on the removable memory card, and using a secure boot invalidating firmware are the physical measures you can use to harden the security of your device.

REAL-WORLD INCIDENTS WHERE IOT DEVICES WERE COMPROMISED

- A widespread incident where IoT devices were compromised occurred with an intelligent security camera. Here, the Xiaomi Mijia camera was in the middle of this incident and got involved in a privacy breach incident where a user reported receiving different images from other people's homes on his Google Nest Hub. This incident brings to question the security of smart home devices and the possible implications such breaches could have on their victims.
- Another incident that brought the world's attention to the realities of IoT device compromises is the Jeep Cherokee hack, and security researchers demonstrated the possibility of gaining remote control over a Jeep Cherokee through zero-day vulnerability. When the Jeep Cherokee is successfully hacked, its breaking and steering systems can be manipulated, which shows the potential danger associated with the vehicle's supposed cutting-edge technology.
- We can't leave this without discussing the Mirai Botnet in 2016. There was a massive DDoS attack by Mirai Botnet through the exploitation of vulnerable IoT devices such as

DVRs and cameras. Major websites fall victim to these attacks, which affect services; this is proof of the potentially destructive capability of the IoT Botnet.

METHODS TO PROTECT INTERCONNECTED DEVICES

There are several methods you can use to protect interconnected devices, and they include:

1. Track and manage your devices: managing devices across an organization can be difficult, especially when you need to know what the devices do and how each works. The first step you must take in securing your IoT infrastructure is to have a good understanding of the connected devices within your organization. The best way to go about managing devices is to consider implementing continuous monitoring software, which can help track, discover, manage, and monitor devices to prevent your organization from any potential future attacks.

2. Patching and remediation: this method allows you to change the code of your connected devices after using them for a while to fortify their security. While implementing a networked device, you must consider whether it can be patched over time to ensure your device can deal with the ever-evolving cyber threats. However, some devices are limited in capabilities or too complex to patch. That is why you need to consider the remediation before implementing a new IoT device onto your network.

3. Updating credentials and passwords has long been in practice and may seem obsolete. However, many devices shipped out often have a vendor-supplied default password. When cybercriminals get access to these passwords, they can use them to gain control of IoT devices to exploit them. That is why maintaining good password hygiene is very important, and you can do this by updating credentials and passwords. It is a necessary step towards your device's routine management to ensure it is secure around the clock.

4. Use the latest encryption protocols: When data are unencrypted, cybercriminals can quickly gain access to steal sensitive information or even intercept communication on the network. Using the latest encryption protocols to encrypt data allows data with the network to be inaccessible to unauthorized users, leaving them secure.

5. Carry out penetration testing or evaluation: The purpose of manufacturing connected devices, which is the ease of use, makes them vulnerable to attacks. Therefore, Organizations must conduct a penetration test or evaluation on their software, hardware, and other equipment before using them for IoT devices. Doing so would help you identify and understand the existing vulnerabilities, regulatory compliance, risk response, employee security, and more. It protects the organization from any serious IoT future threat.

6. Understand your endpoints more clearly: when a new IoT device comes on board, a new endpoint also comes into the network. You can introduce endpoint by adding smartphones, a new laptop, cloud-based server printers, etc. So, with each endpoint that is created, it is also a potential entry point for cybercriminals.

The ever-increasing number of devices connecting to corporate networks makes it more challenging to control all devices in the network, making organizations need help to maintain adequate endpoint security. Therefore, your organization understands, identifies, and profiles its IoT endpoint to have a secure network and have a better understanding of how to improve your endpoint security; your organization can leverage tools such as endpoint security tools that offer mobile device management, data encryption, security patch updates, antivirus updates and so on.

7. Have your network segmented: you have to look ahead into the future and be conscious that your devices might get hacked when integrating IoT devices into your network. This is to help you be better prepared and well-tooled for any eventual breach. Relying on a segmented network allows your organization to deal with attacks better by splitting computer networks into sub-network series. With segmentation, your organization can effectively control unauthorized users from one network to another before getting a chance to infect the next. Also, you can minimize the point of access to sensitive data for the various applications in the segmented area.

8. Using multi-factor authentication: this form is a notch higher than the standard two-factor authentication. With multi-factor authentication, users must give two or more verifiable factors before accessing an IoT device. By doing this, you can improve the security and health of your network by adding an extra layer of protection from cyber-attacks.

THE IMPORTANCE OF REGULAR SOFTWARE UPDATES AND STRONG NETWORK SECURITY PRACTICES

What comes to your mind each time you hear IoT update management? Update management oversees and executes updates for various IoT devices. Its main aim is to keep devices safe, efficient, and updated with recent improvements and features. The performances and longevity of IoT devices can be improved for manufacturers and users through effective update management.

THE ROLE OF USER AWARENESS AND BEHAVIOR IN IOT SECURITY

- **Understanding risks:** users need to be conscious of possible security risks that come with IoT devices, including device manipulation, unauthorized access to personal data, and hacking.
- **Help set up a secure configuration:** The user must use best practices when setting up and configuring IoT devices safely. The best practices may include enabling encryption, keeping firmware/software up to date, and changing default passwords.
- **Privacy concerns:** privacy is essential, and users must be conscious of their privacy and its implications on IoT devices. Privacy concerns may be about sharing personal information, data collection services, and consent to use data.
- **Avoid leaving default settings:** users must resist the practice of leaving default settings on their IoT devices. Leaving default settings on it can cause them to be vulnerable to attacks.
- **Frequent and prompt updates and maintenance:** users must frequently and promptly update their IoT devices and learn to maintain them to patch their Vulnerabilities and keep them safe from attacks.
- **Social engineering attacks awareness:** Users need to be cautious about social engineering attacks that seek to cause them to reveal sensitive details that can be used to access their IoT devices.
- **Physical security measures:** users also need to consider physical security measures for their various IoT devices.

The physical security measures could be keeping the IoT devices in places where they are secure and untempered.

FUTURE TRENDS IN IOT CYBERSECURITY

Some trends have been predicted to be the new possible sides of IoT cybersecurity to come, and they are:

1. Increase AI support for IoT: the IEEE survey showed that respondents indicated that the top four possible AI applications in the coming years will center on real-time cybersecurity, attack prevention, vulnerability identification, accelerated software development and automated customer service, warehouse authorization efficiency, and increased supply chain. However, warehouse automation efficiency will need significant investment in IoT technology to aid development, product identification, and handling.

Factories with IoT-capable technologies can facilitate local intelligence and extensive monitoring alongside automation and robotics to cease operations that could have required several people working closely together to achieve the same task. Thanks to the brilliance of IoT-based systems, people are continuously filling roles where they can use their unique capabilities to make the best decisions through subjective or objective criteria combined with machine intelligence to create an efficient and more secure factory.

2. Increased connectivity for IoT devices with a broader reach: according to IoT analytics on the May 2023 report tagged, State of IoT– Spring 2023, it was projected that the growth of IoT devices would hit 27 billion by 2025. The increased replacement of 2G/3G networks with 4G/5G would help facilitate this growth.

3. **Cost-effective IoT Product Components:** There are possibilities for gradually relieving the chip shortage as more production lines come on board. However, there was an oversupply of other chips in 2023, including NAND flash memories and dynamic RAM (DRAM), which led to a drastic price slash. With lower prices and increased availability of components in the coming years, it will likely cut down on the costs of endpoint IoT products, which will encourage its adoption in more sectors.

4. **Improved technological innovations:** IoT encourages cutting-edge technological innovations to drive future growth. These technological innovations could include a shift in the architectural designs of computers. The significant drivers are changes in memory approaches and storage, which can affect how we process and store data at the network endpoints. As a result, limited data is transferred with lower processing power. Also, with a new form of chipset packaging technology, we can have a denser and more specialized chip-based system, which includes your endpoints, IoT devices, and network edge. Also, switching some volatile to nonvolatile memory is possible, where IoT devices with more incredible memory can store and process data at lower processing power. Fundamental changes applied to computer processing can impact IoT applications in the future.

5. **System disaggregation allows for more efficient data processing.** With the disaggregation of the traditional data center servers and the introduction of a virtual computing system, we can have more efficient data processing with less power, making computing more sustainable. Most data processed at the data center are from the IoT application, and as it grows, so does the processing. The Compute Express Link(CXL) and Nonvolatile Memory Express (NVMe), coupled with the improvements they bring to computer designs, can reduce the cost of many IoT applications.

6. Modern chip design and set standards: with the introduction of triplet, the traditional semiconductor designs are disaggregating by themselves. The current chipset separates most of the conventional CPU functions into more minor, interconnected chips to generate high speed on small packages. A chip standard named the Universal Chiplet Interconnect Express (UCle) was introduced in 2022 to bring about specialized chips from many manufacturers to combine them in a compact package. This allows for more production of specialized semiconductor chipset packages for particular kinds of applications and also creates a need for modern foundries to assemble chips into UCLe packages, which will bring about a more efficient semiconductor for network edges, IoT endpoint devices, and data centers.

7. New and developing persistent or nonvolatile memory technologies for IoT: when the costs of NAND flash, DRAM, and another essential semiconductor for IoT devices are lower, an increase in memory density can not only help in lowering costs but also allow an increase in the capabilities of IoT devices. New and persistent or nonvolatile memory technologies appear in IoT devices specifically for code storage in designs below 28nm. For example, resistive and magnetic RAM (RRAM and MRAM) can find their use in consumer IoT devices. Using MRAM instead of RAM demands lower processing power, especially when the IoT device is inactive and in use. For devices that are energy-constrained, this could be of a more significant advantage.

FUTURE CHALLENGES AND OPPORTUNITIES IN IOT SECURITY

- **Lack of visibility:** IT departments are often not aware when users decide to deploy their IoT devices, which makes it difficult to track inventory of what should be monitored or needed.
- **Partial security integration:** given the size and scale of the IoT devices, it becomes challenging and sometimes impossible to integrate IoT devices into the security system.
- **Vulnerabilities due to open-source code:** today, many firmware developed for IoT devices contain software from open-source and carry bugs that could compromise network and IoT systems.
- **Massive volume of data:** the overwhelming quantity of data generated using IoT devices makes management, protection, and data oversight more difficult.
- **Weak Passwords:** IoT devices come ready with their default passwords, and many users often fail to change them. This makes the IoT devices vulnerable and could cause them to suffer an attack from cybercriminals. Also, users make the mistake of creating weak and guessable passwords.
- **Vulnerabilities in APIs:** attacker often uses APIs as attack entry points. The attackers can gain access to the command and control centers to carry out their malicious attacks, such as man-in-the-middle (MITM), distributed denial of service (DDOS) network breaches, and SQL injection.

- **Unpatched Vulnerabilities:** most IoT devices come with unpatched Vulnerabilities for various reasons, such as unavailable patches or difficulty installing and accessing patches.
- **Inadequate testing:** most IoT developers are less concerned about security and fail to conduct vulnerability tests to detect weaknesses in the IoT systems.

QUIZ

1. Does the role of user awareness and behavior in IoT security include all except?

    a) Understanding risks
    b) Concerns for privacy
    c) Social Security
    d) Social engineering attack awareness.

2. _____ is a future trend in IoT cybersecurity

    a) Improved innovation technology
    b) Patches
    c) Cyber endpoints
    d Attacks

3. IoT devices often come with default passwords. True/false?

4. DRAM is a type of _____

5. Will the practice of patching APIs regularly mitigate Vulnerabilities? Yes/No.

As we've seen, securing our interconnected devices is just the beginning. The next step in our cybersecurity journey takes us into threat intelligence and proactive defense, where staying one step ahead of cyber threats is vital.

THREAT INTELLIGENCE AND PROACTIVE DEFENSE

Presently, cyber threats can come from anywhere; we must rethink our safety when operating in this digital space and must have ingrained in our minds that security isn't just about having an impenetrable wall but also being able to tell where the next attack might be coming from. In this chapter, you will have the proper knowledge to help you detect any cyber threats before they can even strike.

EXPLORING CYBERTHREAT INTELLIGENCE

Today, we can predict weather patterns and accurately tell what they will be in certain places and periods. All these weather pattern reports are possible with the knowledge of weather forecasting. Now think of your cyber threat Intelligence in the same way as weather forecasting: being able to tell something will happen before it occurs.

Threat Intelligence or cyber threat Intelligence is a form of knowledge centered around cybersecurity. The need for cyber threat Intelligence is drawn from various sources' concerns about prevailing cyber threats to identify and tell if a potential attack lurks. Threat Intelligence would help you determine the attack behaviors of a threat actor, their target, and the motives behind them, and also take steps to implement fortified defenses to prevent such attacks in the future. According to reports, the IBM data breach 2022 cost victims about $4.35 million, giving you an idea of the consequences of a failed cyber threat Intelligence. But with successful cyber threat intelligence, you can avoid these losses and prevent them from being attacked altogether.

Threat Intelligence can benefit Organizations in various ways, including

- Improved threat detection and better decision-making: with threat Intelligence, your ability to detect is improved. You can also monitor threats using powerful tools to help you make better and more accurate security decisions for your Organization.
- More effective threat response: cyber threat Intelligence can provide detailed information about the techniques, tactics, and procedures (TTPs) used by threat actors and the possible indicators of compromise (IoCs) of the cyber attacks. Security teams can pick up this information and use it to remediate threats or address any persisting vulnerabilities.
- Helps address the Organization's specific threats: cyber threat Intelligence is not only concerned with general malware but can also be tailored to particular vulnerabilities existing in the Organization's attack surface. You can prioritize incidents according to their risk

and impact on the Organization. Also, you must consider factors such as the type of attack and what assets were affected.
- Actionable suggestions and automated processes: machine learning capabilities coupled with threat history data allow for automatic detection and block. At the same time, the system gives valuable insights and suggestions for your defense through analyzing data.

TYPES OF THREAT INTELLIGENCE

- **Strategic threat Intelligence:** this type of Intelligence gives a high level of information, especially to the desk of senior leadership within the Organization, to help them make decisions concerning the existing threats. Strategic threat Intelligence deals with non-technical aspects of information, which makes it unnecessary to collect data continuously.
- **Technical threat intelligence:** this type of Intelligence allows security teams to collect information from its Intelligence feeds. Security teams can use this type of threat intelligence to investigate a security incident or watch emerging threats.
- **Operational threat intelligence:** this type of threat intelligence allows security teams to have information that will help them get to action to counter any threat actor, the motive, and timing, and help them to implement measures to detect an attack or prevent it altogether proactively.

- **Tactical threat intelligence:** in this type of threat intelligence, you will have a better focus on malicious actors' techniques, tactics, and procedures (TTPs) and even have a better insight into potential attacks, the way and manner in which malicious actors could compromise an organization IT environment.

IMPORTANCE OF UNDERSTANDING THREAT LANDSCAPE

The threat landscape involves factors that carry risk to individual entities in their various context. These contexts represent specific elements that could affect the level of risk posed to a particular industry, Organization, time, or user group, such as:

- The level of information security present
- The value of available sensitive information
- Geopolitical factors: a threat could come from actors from different countries or geographical locations and launch their targets upon individuals or groups from specific countries or geography like the Advanced Persistent Threat. (APTs).

REAL-LIFE EXAMPLES OF THREAT INTELLIGENCE OPERATIONS

1. **Botnet Attacks:** Threat intelligence can help you identify and respond to Botnet Attacks. It does this by giving details about the attacker's technique, tactics, and procedures. Still, with threat Intelligence, you're better guided on remediation efforts and strategies for recovery.

This would help the Organization create more effective techniques to reduce any chances of an attack.
2. **Surge in Ransomware:** When organizations experience a rise in ransomware, threat intelligence allows them to target training their employees to recognize and equally respond to such threats. This enhances the Organization's overall security outlook and mitigates the risks of a cyber attack.

TECHNIQUES AND TOOLS FOR CYBER THREAT HUNTING

Imagine a police detective trying to weed out a criminal from within a population. The criminal uses the rest of the other people to camouflage. When no one is watching, they repeat their crime repeatedly. But a brilliant detective has the knowledge and skills to identify and take out the criminal no matter how they may want to hide their identity. This is how cyber threat hunting works, too, except that the cyber systems are a stack here, and threats must be identified and dealt with accordingly.

Think of threat hunting as a practice that allows you to search for cyber threats proactively, camouflaging inside your network. But with cyber hunting, you can dig deeper to find any malicious actor within your cyberspace who initially got past other endpoint security defenses.

As soon as an attacker gains entry into your network, they will hide in the background for months while collecting data undetected, searching out for sensitive materials, or even having access to login credentials, allowing them to navigate the network environment.

STANDARD TOOLS AND TECHNIQUES USED IN THREAT HUNTING

1. **An analytical-driven tool** uses a behavioral pattern coupled with machine learning threat hunting to develop risk scores and other possible probes. Examples of analytics-driven tools are Cuckoo Soundbox, Automated, and Maltego CE.
2. **Intelligence-driven tools:** with this tool, you can collect data, and with an existing report, you can use them both in your threat hunting. Examples of such devices are CrowdFMS, BotScout, and YARA.
3. **Situation Awareness-driven tools:** Crown Jewel and risk assessment analysis are often used to evaluate individual or company trends. In turn, it shows.
4. **The level of present risks:** Examples of situational Awareness-driven tools include YETI and AI Engine.

Other Hunting Tools Include:

1. **IBMX-Force Exchange:** This is a threat-hunting platform that combines both machine learning and human capabilities to search for threats throughout the entire cyber system, collect actionable data, consult with experts, and collaborate with peers. If you want to stay ahead in the world of cyber threats, this platform is what you should look into for yourself.
2. **Skyhawk:** this functions to alert the security operations team with real-time alerts concerning related events, which is developed into a storyline. It allows you to analyze events and help you study their progress to stall false positive signals. Every activity is arranged into a story

and given a risk score. When the score gets to a particular point, it alerts the SOC team, saving their time and allowing them to focus on accurate alerts, not false positives. This can come in handy for especially cloud-based companies and their security team.

3. **Memcyco:** this offers authentication solutions that help customers and partners trust that the message you sent them is from you and safe to open. All required is a single line of code, a landing page, or a webpage that gets an authentication. When hackers try to duplicate the site or phish users, you will receive an alert in real-time to allow you to take quick action. This can be very useful for your Organization if it wants to be proactive about securing customers' trust.

4. **SpectralOPs:** with SpectralOPs, you can protect your infrastructure's vulnerable and high-risk assets. You can do this by automatically embedding secret protection within your infrastructure. You can also monitor it to identify the gaps and blindspots, establish your policies, and build your detectors in developing your software. This can be very useful for both DevOps and software developers.

5. **Trend Micro:** It offers extended detection and response (XDR) using different techniques and bringing them into a platform. It aims to help improve your system's speed and accuracy in detecting cyber threats. Using third-party inputs, easy search options, and deep activity data from internal and external information (third party), coupled with an interactive graph, you can prioritize according to the immediate importance and then set your architectural response on automation. This can be useful for companies and enterprises.

6. **Jit:** traditionally, Jit.io is not recognized as a hunting tool, but it can help track the threats hidden in codes. It is not a robust security platform and allows developers to own security for their products from the get-go. Also, it helps engineers navigate security issues when building codes by compiling all necessary information into a single platform. The engineering teams in software companies can derive plenty from this tool.
7. **CrowdStrike:** CrowdStrike is a hunting tactic that goes the extra mile in detection: it can detect the 1% of threats that usually evade detection with other tools. It combines several devices, such as sensors that oversee millions of endpoints before being categorized for easy visibility and an almost real-time threat intelligence using human experiences and skills. When a CrowdStrike detects a threat, it brings it into a context to help you understand and give you actionable insight to take the best and quickest approach. All organizations of various sizes can use this tool to improve their cyber threat detection.
8. **CybeReady:** just like Jit.io, CybeReady is not a threat-hunting solution like the others. However, it brings in some critical components that most hunting tools overlook: the human element. It allows for security awareness training by offering an extensive security program, audit tools, compliance tools, and phishing simulations. Such a tool will relieve IT departments of a great deal of burden with its user-friendly interface. Therefore, IT managers, cybersecurity team managers, heads of IT, and CISOs in various companies and organizations can use this tool to improve their security awareness among employees.
9. **VMware:** VMware allows several security endpoint capabilities with billions more system events to come into

a single console, which helps select the standard in your environment. With these features, VMware has a minor fluctuation that could signify a malicious attack. A more advanced cyber attack strategy offers an automated response workflow that allows you to act more effectively and efficiently and helps you to get back to your regular activities as soon as possible.

MORE CYBER THREAT HUNTING TOOLS:

1. Cyberchef: this threat hunting tool was released in 2016 by a secretive agency known as GCHQ and is well-known across the security profession. The Cyberchef is a tool designed to analyze and decode data. It was very elaborate in its scope when it first launched, but today, it has even grown more in capabilities. It doesn't matter if you choose to decode Base64, XOR, or some other exotic, such as the Bacon Cipher; Cyberchef is capable and would do it quickly. It can also detect many different types of encoding nested in data.

Still, it isn't about Cyberchef; the authors are tirelessly working to enhance its forensic, language, and networking capabilities. The most critical aspect of this platform is its recipe function, which gives hunters the power to chain operations, input, and output and bring them all together into recipes.

2. Phishing catcher: There could be no other reason this tool was introduced than that phishing remains a significant threat to most organizations. Most hunters highly recommend it in managing phishing attacks. It is an open-source tool that detects phishing domains in real-time. It relies on suspicious data issued TLS certificates in real-time. A CertStream public API then publishes the data from a Certificate Transparency Log (CTL). Then, the phishing catcher parses the data by looking for user-defined keywords and marking the outcomes. The keywords may include a trademark, an organization's name, or any suspicious term. Phishing catcher also comes with scoring based on specific criteria, allowing hunting teams to have all eyes on the real threats.

3. RSS Readers: it stands for straightforward syndication (RSS) reader and is more than a threat-hunting tool. Instead, we can best describe it as A threat-hunting tool category. For a more successful hunt, hunters must keep up with news updates about Vulnerabilities and patches. But where to find this news is another point of concern. A group of hunters suggested following vendors' sites to get information about Vulnerabilities and patches. Other hunters formed a red team and made exploits on several publishing sites a top priority.

4. GNUPLOT: This hunting tool is an open-source that allows for a two- or three-dimensional representation of data, and it is famous for its rave reviews from threat hunters in 1986.

Threat hunters need data visualization to identify and analyze statistical outliers. While some hunters prefer Excel for this task, many more prefer Gnuplot due to its command line tool against Excel's GUI. With the command line for Gnuplot, hunters can have massive amounts of data and still have instant results outputs. Although it has a powerful interface, the difficulty with it is its steep learning curve.

5. YARA: this is a widespread hunting tool with a fascinating legacy. Although its original purpose was for malware classification, it has become a popular choice for hunters today; it is for no other reason than the YARA ingestible format in which security controls write its rules to detect malware. Several tools are leveraged on YARA, including the YARA generator, which helps threat hunters build YARA rules.

6. AttackerkB: this tool furnishes hunters and adversaries with all they need to understand exploits like disclosure, exploitability, technical analysis, ease of use, outcomes, etc. With such information, hunters can identify and place new and legacy Vulnerabilities using a bottom-up approach. Also, hunters can tell the Vulnerabilities that apply to their respective Organizations.

7. DNSTWIST: This threat-hunting tool helps catch suspicious domains. It is a powerful tool that uses various fuzzing algorithms to Identify questionable parts. DNSTWIST can detect homoglyphs and internalize domain names and mistyped domains. Also, it can identify live phishing and geo-find all results in identifying suspicious outliers.

Still, DNSTWIST can detect rogue MX hosts. This tool can see domains configured to gulp up misdirected emails, which attackers often use to harvest emails or conduct reconnaissance activities.

TIPS FOR BASIC THREAT HUNTING PRACTICES

- **Internal or outsourced:** The first thing you want to do in your threat hunting is know whether to use your internal security team if you have one or outsource your external teams. So, if your Organization lacks the necessary security expertise to handle a threat, outsourcing it to external security teams becomes an option. But when outsourcing your security, you must be cautious about who you're outsourcing them to and how much access you would want them to have.
- **Have a proper plan in place:** whatever decision you have come up with, whether outsourcing your security or maintaining your internal security team, you must have a

proper plan to guide you in executing your security measures to achieve the best results.
- **Select a problem to look deeper into after choosing those who would take charge of your internal security;** the team needs to identify a throbbing problem of the Organization, analyze it, identify its source, and have a clearer understanding.
- **Develop and test your hypothesis:** after analyzing the problem, you can test your hypothesis from the hunt using tools such as WMI and PowerShell.
- **Collect information:** after reviewing your PowerShell activity, you can now collect network information by reviewing network endpoint data or logs, which you can find in database logs, window event logs, or server logs
- **Organize your data:** you need to collect all data from the various sources in your network and put them into an organized format where you can view and make reports. You can use report tools such as SIEM or analytic tools such as Excel to organize your data.
- **Automate routine tasks:** keeping up with repeating the same task over and over can be tiring, which could make you lose track of the threat, leaving your entire ecosystem vulnerable. So, automate the task to get your hands on other important things crucial to the security of your cyber network.
- Get answers to your questions and plan the following action: You must have all the information at this stage. Now, you can answer each of those questions from your probe correctly. From there, you can determine the best action to take.

BUILDING A PROACTIVE CYBERSECURITY STRATEGY

Building a proactive cybersecurity strategy is like having a health plan to help you stay healthy always. It is not enough to have a plan; you must actively put what is planned into practice, and that is where your plan or strategy becomes meaningful. There are several cybersecurity strategies to use, and they include:

- Understanding what you have, what you must protect, and what you're protecting against gives you a picture of what you lack and need to patch up.
- Strong user authentication policies and a zero-trust approach allow you to control those who could access your system or database.
- Make your plan agile and adaptive: your strategy should be such that it is adaptable to any situation you may encounter and be solid enough to wade off attacks effectively.
- Plotting for the future: You want to ensure that your strategy considers the future. So make sure it can tackle threats in the future.
- Look out for impersonators: your plan must be structured to weed out impersonators.
- Hunt for Vulnerabilities/threats: identify the Vulnerabilities and threats that your Organization is faced with.
- Practice responses: You must practice responding to each of the questions developed from your analysis.

HOW TO INCORPORATE THREAT INTELLIGENCE INTO DAILY CYBERSECURITY PRACTICES

1. Choose a suitable source of threat data for your Organization
2. Decide on who will acquire your Organization's data
3. Setup your collected data for analysis
4. Make use of tools to help you in your analysis
5. Pick the most suitable means to set your data into action.

CONTINUOUS NATURE OF CYBERSECURITY

Cybersecurity is not something you get fixed in just one go; it requires a conscious effort and process that demands constant vigilance, attention, and adoption. The cyber threat landscape keeps evolving daily, with ever-new Vulnerabilities coming up regularly. That means individuals and organizations must continuously improve their cybersecurity measures to manage the risks effectively and protect sensitive information.

Regular software updates are vital in helping you maintain a robust cybersecurity defense. Vendor releases updates and patches to take care of a newly identified vulnerability and help fortify your security protocols. Skipping these updates or failing to apply the recently released updates could make your system more vulnerable to cyber attacks; that is why you must have an elaborate patch management process to ensure your software is updated as regularly as it should.

You can only discuss an effective cybersecurity strategy if you mention education; it is fundamental to any cybersecurity strategy. And because cyber threats are becoming more sophisticated, individuals and employees must be updated about emerging and evolving tactics and the best practices they can use to reduce the risks. That means they must attend training programs, simulations, and workshops to improve their awareness of common attack vectors such as malware, social engineering, and phishing. By encouraging a cybersecurity awareness culture, organizations can help their staff and employees identify and effectively respond to potential threats, strengthening their overall security outlook.

Your cybersecurity plan must be adaptable because threat actors are always on an adventure to seek new ways to breach defenses, which makes it all the more necessary for organizations to remain solid and responsive to new threats. That means you may have to constantly reassess and update security policies, carry out a thorough risk assessment, and invest in new technologies such as machine learning and artificial intelligence to identify and promptly reduce cyber-attack risks.

CROSSWORDS

1. There are _____ types of threat intelligence
2. IoC stands for _____
3. Maltego is an example of an Analytics-driven tool. T/F
4. Agile and adaptive are part of the elements of proactive cybersecurity. T/F
5. An example of a real-life threat intelligence is _____ a. Botnet attack b. Maltego C. IoC d. Malware

Armed with knowledge about threat intelligence and proactive defense, let's look ahead to the future of cybersecurity. The next chapter will explore emerging trends and how to stay prepared in an ever-evolving digital landscape.

Judging from where you stand, where do you think cybersecurity will lead us in the next decade? In this chapter, we will glance into the future of cybersecurity, discussing the challenges and innovations ahead.

EMERGING TRENDS AND TECHNOLOGIES

The cost of cyberattacks on the global economy has been predicted to be $ 10.5 trillion by the end of 2024. This outrageous amount shows why we must prioritize our cybersecurity on individual, government, and organizational levels.

Like in all technological endeavors and businesses, AI will have a transformative impact on attack and defense that will most likely be felt in the trends I'm about to show you.

Technological development is accelerated across many fields and is the level of cyber threat. It is wise always to stay ahead and prepared, and knowing the cybersecurity trends is a way to help you achieve that.

1. Cybersecurity in the board room: the strategic priority of cybersecurity can no longer be left in the hands of those in the IT department alone. Just like Gartner predicted, about 70 percent of boards will need at least an IT expert by 2026 so that organizations can go beyond the reactive kind of defense. That's to say, these organizations can take on new opportunities with business while actively preparing against any cyber eventuality.

2. Next-level phishing attacks: Attackers use social engineering to trick users into giving them access to the system, and this form of attack will become even more sophisticated. With the advent of generative AI, attackers can make smarter, deepfake, and more personalized attack approaches, which will also become more prevalent. Organizations need to invest in education and awareness in response to these attacks. However, zero trust and AI would play a more significant role.

3. Cyber resilience-beyond cybersecurity: cybersecurity and cyber resilience are two terms most often used interchangeably. But their differences would become more pronounced in 2024 and beyond. While cybersecurity is centered on preventing attacks, the ever-increasing value on resilience cultivated by most organizations tells a hard reality that no matter how challenging the level of security may be, there is no 100 percent guarantee of protection. Resilience measures are established to allow for continuous operation even in the case of a successful cyber breach. Being capable of bouncing back more intensely and mitigating downtime and data loss will be a strategic priority in the future.

4. IoT Cyberattacks: with more linkages among devices and increased internet connectivity, there are more excellent potential openings that cyberattacks can exploit, and with the evolution of work where more people go increasingly remote, there are heightened risks in connecting and sharing data over unsecured devices, and it is a big concern. Most of the time, these devices are more about ease of use and convenience than secure operation, and remote users of these IoT devices are at much greater risk due to their poor security plans and weak passwords. Despite the delay in implementing IoT security standards, even while the vulnerabilities have become more evident over the years, we will continue to see it as a cybersecurity problem. However, there are hopes that it may change.

5. Cyber warfare and state-sponsored cyberattacks: the Russian-Ukraine war has run into its third year now and has shown to the world how far states can go in deploying cyberattacks against civilian and military infrastructure. This has opened up a new discussion that each time there is a military operation around the world, there is the possibility of a cyberattack. A common tactic includes phishing attacks tailored to access systems to destroy and spy and distributed denial-of-service attacks to turn off public utilities, security infrastructure, transport systems, and communications. Other than warfare, it is also expected that these kind of attacks may find their way into our election in the coming years to disrupt democratic processes.

6. Less than zero trust: the basic concept of zero trust is always; verification keeps evolving as systems become more complex by the day and security is being strategically integrated into the business. Zero trust allows us to assume that there is no perimeter in which we should assume that our network activity is safe. The more expanded threat landscape is the zero trust principle, which goes beyond the corporate network and onto the network of those working remotely, IoT devices, and partnered organizations. Zero trust is expected to move from a technical network security model to a more holistic and adaptive type that allows for continuous AI-powered activity monitoring and real-time authentication in the coming years.

7. Cybersecurity regulation: cybersecurity continues to be a significant national security concern for both government and private organizations, and the threat it poses to the economy's growth. Also, the potential risk of data breaches in the social and political atmosphere is a significant consideration in cybersecurity regulations. For instance, businesses across the UK have a grace period until April 2024 to make sure their operations comply with the Telecommunication Act and product security, which has been set as a minimum security requirement networked products are expected to adhere to, like not shipping products with a default password. Another regulation expected to usher a change in the cybersecurity landscape but is being delayed until 2025 is the implementation of the similar Radio Equipment Directive. Still, the discussion will likely be a top agenda for legislators all through 2024.

8. Automotive cybersecurity threats: modern vehicles have cutting-edge features such as sophisticated software, seamless connectivity, driver assistant systems, engine timing, and cruise control. But all these features rely on connectivity and automation, which could expose vehicles to hacking risks. Technologies such as WiFi and Bluetooth allow hackers to exploit existing vulnerabilities and gain access to vehicle controls or even spy on picks in the conversation using built-in microphones. More vehicles are increasingly adapted to this cutting-edge technology, thereby heightening the risks of a threat. Stricter security measures are necessary for autonomous or self-driving cars.

9. Artificial intelligence in cybersecurity: AI has played a critical role in various industry sectors. With the aid of machine learning algorithms, AI has pushed the development of Automated cybersecurity to a whole new level and can adapt to natural language processing tasks, threat detection, and face recognition. Still, AI technology is leveraged by malicious hackers to carry out sophisticated attacks to gain access to systems. Even with these threats, AI offers tools that can help you respond to these threats promptly and serve as a critical support tool to cybersecurity professionals.

10. Mobile Devices: mobile devices are increasingly becoming a target for most cyberattacks. The proliferation of these devices makes them all the more attractive for cybercriminals, especially with increased personal and mobile banking targeted attacks and malware. Today, smartphones are used everywhere and in almost all kinds of activities, from financial transactions to communication, which heightens the risks of potential breaches. Mobile security has become an essential topic of discussion as cyber threats evolve, with trends showing that smartphone-specific malware and viruses are on the rise.

11. cloud security and solutions Issues: Organizations rely more on cloud services than ever. That means the need for robust security measures becomes even more critical for its data storage and operations. Although most cloud providers ensure they implement a strong security protocol, there may still be some Vulnerabilities from malicious software, phishing attacks, or user-end errors. That is why it is essential to constantly monitor and update software to reduce the risks of attacks and protect the confidentiality of your data stored in the cloud.

12. Data Breaches: this remains a persistent concern among individuals and organizations throughout the globe, and just a minor flaw in software can render your whole system vulnerable. However, regulatory frameworks such as CCPA and GDPR try to solve these with enhanced privacy rights and data protection, prompting the need for more stringent security measures. Keeping to this regulation's provisions and putting proactive security measures in place is necessary to mitigate the impact of any data breaches.

13. 5G evolution and IoT security: the 5G evolution is bringing a new experience in speed to our cyber world and interconnectivity, especially with IoTs. However, the 5G brings almost seemlessness in connectivity but opens IoT devices up to Vulnerabilities from software bugs and external threats. The 5G technology is still very new, meaning more research is necessary to find and deal with potential Vulnerabilities lurking in it. Therefore, manufacturers must consider developing software and hardware less prone to cybersecurity issues like network attacks and data breaches.

14. Adoptions of authorization for improved cybersecurity: the ever-growing data size can better be managed with authorization, which can help streamline our data security processes. Automation can be a valuable support tool for most security professionals, allowing them to respond swiftly and efficiently to potential threats. So, strategically placing your security measures into a robust development process brings more secure software solutions for more extensive and complex applications.

15. Ransomware attacks: These attacks are significant to industries relying on particular software systems and have enormous consequences. A recent cyber attack like the Wannacry attack on healthcare institutions shows how vital a robust cybersecurity plan must be. Therefore, an organization must remain watchful against Ransomware threats and implement proactive measures to mitigate the risks effectively.

16. Prevalence of state-sponsored cyber warfare: The tension between global powers has caused state-sponsored cyber warfare targeted at sensitive data or critical support infrastructure. Events like elections are also unsafe from these cyber threats, making all-encompassing security measures more than necessary. In 2024, there is expected to be a surge in state-sponsored actors and data breaches with interests in exploiting industrial and political data.

17. Managing threats from within through awareness: individual mistakes from within the organization contribute considerably to data breaches, and they can become more severe with an insider working for malicious external hackers. To deal with these risks, you must introduce awareness programs through employee training. When your employees are well aware of the potential dangers and Vulnerabilities that can be exploited, they can identify and address them quickly while fostering a more robust cybersecurity culture. This approach is necessary for safeguarding data assets and reducing the impact of the threats from Within.

18. Cybersecurity challenges in the remote work environment: Ever since the pandemic and the transition into remote work, persistent and new cybersecurity issues keep coming up as employees browse unsecured networks. Organizations must prioritize the implementation of solid security protocols like a secure VPN and multi+factor authentication to protect remote workers effectively from cyber threats.

19. Countering social engineering attacks: Until now, attacks such as phishing and identity theft have been a significant cause of concern for most organizations that rely on human vulnerabilities to gain malicious access to sensitive information. Dealing with social engineering attack risks requires proactive security measures and employee training.

20. Improving cybersecurity with multi-factor authentication: with multi-factor authentication, you will have an additional layer of security that demands users to provide multiple authentications before they can have full access to an account or system. This approach limits unauthorized access and strengthens the overall cybersecurity outlook. Therefore, organizations must adopt multi-factor authentication to protect their networks or systems against cyber threats effectively.

21. Protecting systems and networks against International state-sponsored attacks: Organizations are constantly threatened by complex state-sponsored attacks targeting sensitive data and critical infrastructure. Proactive security measures such as multi-factor authentication and real-time monitoring are necessary in fighting against these threats.

22. Strengthening Identity and Access Management: effective identity and access management policies can help Organizations to have control and access over sensitive data and networks. Having all-encompassing access control, authorization, and authentication measures Is vital in protecting against data breaches and unauthorized access.

23. Monitoring data in real-time to detect threats early: With real-time data monitoring, organizations can detect and respond to suspicious activity as it surfaces, which can help reduce the risk of cyberattacks and data breaches. Activating automated alerts and log monitoring are essential in helping to identify potential threats and minimize their impact.

24. Protecting connected vehicles against cyber threats: Many cars are fitted with connectivity, which could be an open spot for cyber threats. It makes it necessary to have robust security measures to protect against potential cyberattacks. Using real-time monitoring, authentication, and encryption, you can effectively secure connected vehicles against automotive hacking.

EVOLUTION OF CYBER THREAT

We have seen a dramatic increase in cyber threats over the past decades. Our digital age has undoubtedly opened doors to new opportunities for growth and innovation but also brings new exploits for cybercriminals. New technologies like AI have allowed attackers to become more sophisticated in their operations.

Here, we will have a look back at the evolution of cyber threats in the past decades, and they are:

2009-2012: the rise of advanced and persistent threats (APTs)

The years between 2009 and 2012 ushered an era in which we saw a rise in advanced persistent threats. The APTs are attacks that happen over a long term, focus on stealing data from specific sources, and are very sophisticated forms of attack. Often, the attacker spends many months or even years collecting sensitive information about the target they will launch their attack upon without being detected.

One such example of this kind of attack happened in 2010. During the attack, Google and other companies were the center of a series of APT attacks known today as Operation Aurora. During the attack, intellectual property and sensitive data were stolen through exploiting vulnerabilities in the company's software system.

Ways to stay safe against APT attacks include a secure VPN, a next-generation firewall, an intrusion prevention system, threat intelligence, and user behavior analytics (UBA).

2013-2016: ransomware and Business Email Compromise (BEC):

There was a spike in ransomware and Business Email Compromise (BEC) attacks in 2013- 2016. While attacker uses ransomware, a type of malware to encrypt a victim's files and demand compensation for a decryption key, BEC involves impersonating a senior executive and deceiving employees into releasing funds into unsuspecting but fraudulent accounts.

Ransomware has been a lucrative cybercrime for cybercriminals, with payments hitting billions of dollars yearly. Also, BEC attacks are rising daily, with an estimated loss from an FBI report placed at $1.7 billion in 2019.

A famous incident, the WannaCry ransomware attack, affected hundreds of thousands of computers, cutting across 150 countries. Often, the attacker demands payment as ransom in exchange for unlocking the successfully attacked systems. Another example at about the same time was the CEO Fraud that happened in 2015, and the tech company, Ubiquiti's Network, came under BEC attack, costing it $46.7 million. The attacker impersonated Ubiquiti executives and tricked the employees into transferring massive sums into overseas accounts.

To avoid ransomware and BEC attacks are access control, user awareness training, anti-malware, email filtering, backup, and recovery.

2017 – 2020: Artificial Intelligence (AI) and Internet of Things (IoT) threats

From 2017 to 2020, we saw increased threats to artificial intelligence and the Internet of Things. We realized this type of attack for the first time within this time frame. The increasing use of IoT devices for remote and onsite business makes them all the more attractive and a lucrative target for cybercriminals. Poor security measures make these devices vulnerable to attacks.

Artificial intelligence contributes to the evolution and sophistication of cyber threats. While it is true that AI plays an important role when deployed in businesses to improve security measures, such as identifying potential threats and detecting abnormal behavior, cybercriminals are also using the same AI to carry out sophisticated attacks.

Today, cybercriminals can use AI to generate phishing emails that look too true to be suspected, which can trick their intended victims into giving out their sensitive information. Also, AI is used to create deep fake audio and videos, which can be used for social engineering attacks.

A massive Maria Botnet cyberattack occurred in 2017, with lots of IoT devices compromised and turned into a network of bots that were then used to launch DDoS attacks on several websites. The botnets were targeted at vulnerable IoT devices such as routers, DVRs, and security cameras that often come with their default login credentials, which are weak to protect against hacking.

An example of this kind of threat was the DeepLocker of 2018. AI-powered malware was created to bypass traditional cybersecurity measures using AI algorithms to conceal and remain undetected until it achieves its aim.

The malware was designed only to activate when it detects a target, like a human's voice or face. The malware was an experiment by IBM's X-Force team and created as a proof-of-concept to show the inherent risks of AI-powered attacks.

Ways to stay safe against an AI attack include device management, machine learning, threat intelligence, behavioral analysis, and network segmentation.

2021 – 2022: Supply chain attacks and ransomware-as-a-service:

2021 and 2022 saw a leap in supply chain attacks and ransomware-as-a-service. On the one hand, the supply chain deals with third-party vendors accessing customer's networks. This attack has been recorded to be very successful, allowing cyber-criminals to target cloud providers, IT companies, and software providers.

Raas is a type of attack where ransomware is rented out to other cybercriminals for a percentage return in profit. Such a business model allows cybercriminals free reign to launch attacks, which spiked ransomware attacks globally, and the SonicWall reports have shown that there were more than 304.7 million ransomware attacks in the first half of 2021 alone, which is about 151 percent rise from a similar period in 2020.

An incident related to this type of attack happened in 2020. The SolarWind supply chain was attacked, affecting many U.S. corporations and government agencies. The attacker exploited SolarWinds vulnerability by compromising its software updates and using them to distribute malware to SolarWinds customers.

Also, ransomware attacks occurred in 2021 on the Colonial Pipeline, shutting down a primary fuel pipeline in the USA. After the attack, the attackers demanded ransom payment before Colonial Pipeline restored access.

Some ways to stay safe against supply chain and ransomware-as-a-service attacks include Access control, user awareness training, vulnerability scanning, anti-malware, backup, and recovery.

2022-present: Deep fake and synthetic identity fraud

With deepfake technology, one can create audio recordings and videos that look exactly like humans, which can be used to conduct social engineering attacks or spread misinformation. But synthetic identity fraud is about generating fake IDs using real and fake information.

These attacks are very effective, and cybercriminals find them helpful in creating deep fake technology to impersonate political leaders or top executives to spread misinformation. Also, according to the FBI on the 2022 Internet Crime Report, synthetic identity fraud is on the increase, pulling about $1 billion in losses in 2022

IMPORTANCE OF STAYING INFORMED ABOUT NEW TECHNOLOGIES FOR EFFECTIVE CYBERSECURITY

Staying informed about new technologies goes far beyond knowing the most recent data breaches. Also, it demands being up to date with the rapid changes in the industry, staying abreast of which companies are leading in the information security sector, and knowing who the thought leaders are. Staying up to date with cybersecurity news helps security managers and CISOs ensure that their teams are adequately informed and well aware of emerging threats.

PREDICTIONS FOR THE FUTURE CHALLENGES IN CYBERSECURITY:

- Ransomware evolution: This type of attack is highly likely to become more sophisticated than it used to be, using advanced encryption techniques and AI to get past detection. Historically, we can draw a parallel since the evolution of malware, where we have a recent generation becoming more sophisticated than the previous.
- IoT Vulnerabilities: the more devices we have connected or linked, the higher the chances to exploit the Vulnerabilities in these devices and the systems and networks. This trend is a typical example of the historical pattern of malware used to target popular platforms as they become more common.
- Cloud security challenges: as people seek the need to access more cloud services, there is a likelihood of a spike in cloud-specific attacks that target sensitive data stored in clouds. We can draw a historical parallel from the evolution of attacks targeting centralized databases and systems.

HOW CURRENT TRENDS MIGHT EVOLVE AND IMPACT CYBERSECURITY STRATEGIES

1. Rapid progress in cybersecurity, but there must be more comprehensive access to systems.
2. The crisis of online trust will deteriorate even further.
3. AI and machine learning technologies will go together like a double-edged sword
4. Downsizing of internet fragmentation

5. There will be a conflict between the regulations, experiments, and privacy in the future
6. There will be uncertainty in the metaverse
7. A more significant concern about shifting power dynamics and sovereignty.

THE IMPORTANCE OF ADAPTABILITY AND CONTINUOUS LEARNING IN THE FACE OF THESE CHALLENGES

- The changes In the threats ecosystem need a shift in how companies think about security. The new work culture often exposes businesses to severe threats. A focused organization will adapt its ways of thinking and behavior accordingly.
- We must have known by now that adaptability is essential for a more robust security culture. Therefore, companies and businesses must remain focused on the skills that help employees develop a mindset that helps them treat security as an ever-evolving landscape that accepts reviews regularly instead of the set-and-abandon approach.
- To have a more robust security culture, you must not stop at the basics but go beyond it. You must establish training methods for phishing simulation to align with another form of education that raises employees' awareness about new and evolving security threats and reflects the precise objectives of the business.

PREPARING FOR THE EVOLVING CYBER THREAT LANDSCAPE

- **Conduct a cybersecurity risk assessment:** Conduct a regular risk assessment to ascertain that your cybersecurity measures are threat-proof.
- **Create network access controls:** enable passworded logins and even multi-factor authorization manage access control.
- **Install antivirus and firewall:** antivirus and firewall help your system run background checks on any harmful wares and remove them if need be.
- **Establish a patch management schedule:** updates on software are often released regularly, so ensure you have a schedule that automatically patches your software.
- **Monitor your network traffic regularly:** constantly monitor traffic and identify any irregularities.
- **Create an incident response plan:** develop an incident response plan to guide through processes in any eventuality.
- **Evaluate the physical security of your business:** the structure of your organization must be such that it enhances business operation. Therefore, you need to evaluate the physical security of your business to align with your overall security outlook.
- **Limit your attack surface:** reducing your attack surface makes more sense than doing anything that only causes them to increase.

As we've navigated the complex world of cybersecurity together, from the basics to the cutting edge, it's clear that our digital journey is ever-evolving. As we wrap up, let's reflect on the lessons learned and look ahead confidently, equipped with the knowledge and skills to secure our digital future.

CONCLUSION

Cybersecurity continues to be a significant challenge in the digital world. It may be difficult to achieve or even impossible until you have all the tools and knowledge to deal with the threats. Malicious hackers will stop at nothing to gain access to your network, system, or devices; their selfish aim pushes them forward, and being able to cause havoc to your business is of great reward for them.

As an individual or organization, you have your interest to protect. Not only that, but you also shoulder a great deal of responsibility to safeguard your interests and those who trusted you (customers, clients, and stakeholders). You don't want to let them down. You also aim to make a profit out of your business while still protecting your reputation. Here is the gist: if you do not stand firm, you may lose on both ends, losing your profits with a battered reputation.

So far in this book, I have covered all you need to take charge of your cybersecurity, from the foundation of cybersecurity, where you get to know the basics of the concept of cybersecurity and the essential network took to aid you in keeping your cyberspace safe, as well as grounding your understanding of threats and vulnerability, to the ways and means to secure your clouds and application; where we explored the fundamental of cloud security, strategies to secure cloud environment and data, the basics of application security in software development. We moved on to see identity access and encryption, where we had a comprehensive knowledge of identity and data management, the role of cryptography in cybersecurity, and best practices for authentication, authorization, and data encryption. Again, we moved on to responding to cyber incidents, where we saw a detailed approach to incident response and management. Then, we looked into steps to prepare and respond to cybersecurity incidents. Next, we moved to see governance, compliance, and risk management, where we pressed to understand the security governance framework, compliance with cybersecurity laws and regulations, and the techniques for managing cybersecurity risks. It didn't end there; the Internet of Things is essential, and we delved into securing the Internet of Things (IoT), where we further explored the challenges and solutions in IoT security and the various methods to protect interconnected devices and networks. Then again, we moved on to see threat intelligence and proactive defense, exploring cyber threat intelligence, techniques, and tools for cyber threat hunting and building a proactive cybersecurity strategy. Finally, we ended this book's chapter by peering into the future of cybersecurity, where we look into emerging trends and technologies, predict future challenges in cybersecurity, and prepare for the evolving threat landscape.

After concluding this book, you should be well grounded on how to go about your cybersecurity. Imagine what your business would look like, your reputation, and your profit margin when you're not considering safeguarding your cyberspace and data assets but acting based on knowledge and proactively. Don't read this book alone. Ask your friends and employees to look into it as well, as you would have confirmed its resourcefulness, so don't be stingy; buy one for them or recommend it, as doing so could mean building a solid wall against cyber criminals.

Remember, every step you take towards better cybersecurity practices contributes to a safer digital world for everyone. You can make a difference, not just in your life but in the lives of those around you. Share your knowledge, lead by example, and help build a community that values and understands the importance of cybersecurity. Let's work together to create a more secure digital future for all.

If you find the book highly beneficial, leave a review; doing so would help curious people and seekers of knowledge to be better guided towards having their own.

REFERENCES

(n.d.). Retrieved from AARP: https://www.aarp.org/money/scams-fraud/info-2022/mental-health-impact.html

(n.d.). Retrieved from Indeed: https://www.indeed.com/career-advice/career-development/cyber-security-concepts

Aranza Trevino, Annne Cutler and Darren Guccione. (n.d.). Retrieved from https://www.keepersecurity.com/blog/2023/03/09/the-importance-of-keeping-software-up-to-date/

Baker, K. (n.d.). *Crowdstrike*. Retrieved from https://www.crowdstrike.com/cybersecurity-101/cyberattacks/most-common-types-of-cyberattacks/

Birdsong, T. (n.d.). Retrieved from McAfee: https://www.mcafee.com/blogs/family-safety/7-common-digital-behaviors-that-put-your-familys-privacy-at-risk/

Brook, C. (n.d.). Retrieved from DATAINSIDER: https://www.digitalguardian.com/blog/50-examples-ransomware-attacks-and-their-impacts

CISA. (n.d.). *American Cyber Defense Agency*. Retrieved from https://www.cisa.gov/news-events/news/understanding-anti-virus-software

Cisco. (n.d.). *What is a Firewall*. Retrieved from https://www.cisco.com/c/en/us/products/security/firewalls/what-is-a-firewall.html

Cisco. (n.d.). *What is Network Security*. Retrieved from https://www.cisco.com/c/en/us/upproducts/security/what-is-network-security.html

Heimdal. (n.d.). *Cybersecurity Basics*. Retrieved from https://heimdalsecurity.com/blog/endpoint-security-best-practices/

Trellix. (n.d.). *What is Endpoint Security*. Retrieved from https://www.trellix.com/security-awareness/endpoint/what-is-endpoint-security/

TREND. (n.d.). Retrieved from What are Network Security Basics: https://www.trendmicro.com/en_za/what-is/network-security/network-security-basics.html

Balbix. (n.d.). Cloud Security. Retrieved from https://www.balbix.com/insights/cloud-security/

Cloudlytics. (n.d.). Difference Between Cloud Security and Traditional Security: What You Need to Know. Retrieved from https://cloudlytics.com/difference-between-cloud-security-and-traditional-security-what-you-need-to-know/

EC-Council. (n.d.). Best Cloud Cyber Security Tips. Retrieved from https://www.

eccouncil.org/cybersecurity-exchange/cloud-security/best-cloud-cyber-security-tips/

Palo Alto Networks. (n.d.). 17 Ways to Secure When Deploying Cloud Environments. Retrieved from https://www.paloaltonetworks.com/cyberpedia/17-ways-to-secure-when-deploying-cloud-environments

ImmuniWeb. (n.d.). Top 10 Cloud Security Incidents in 2022. Retrieved from https://www.immuniweb.com/blog/top-10-cloud-security-incidents-in-2022.html

VMware. (n.d.). Application Security. Retrieved from https://www.vmware.com/topics/glossary/content/application-security.html

Forbes Tech Council. (2020, July 16). 14 Expert Tips for Choosing a Secure Messaging App. Forbes. https://www.forbes.com/sites/forbestechcouncil/2020/07/16/14-expert-tips-for-choosing-a-secure-messaging-app/?sh=2bf2cf604ebf

TechTarget. (n.d.). Identity Access Management (IAM) System. Retrieved from https://www.techtarget.com/searchsecurity/definition/identity-access-management-IAM-system

Cybriant. (n.d.). Security Benefits of Identity and Access Management (IAM). Retrieved from https://cybriant.com/security-benefits-of-identity-and-access-management-iam/

Flower, J. (n.d.). Managing Your Digital Identity: Unlocking the Power of Access. Retrieved from https://www.linkedin.com/pulse/managing-your-digital-identity-unlocking-power-access-joe-flower/

Resmo. (n.d.). Access Control Best Practices. Retrieved from https://www.resmo.com/blog/access-control-best-practices

Delinea. (n.d.). Digital Identities: The Future and How We Will Get There. Retrieved from https://delinea.com/blog/digital-identities-the-future-and-how-we-will-get-there

GeeksforGeeks. (n.d.). Cryptography and Its Types. Retrieved from https://www.geeksforgeeks.org/cryptography-and-its-types/

TitanFile. (n.d.). What is Data Encryption and Why is it Important? Retrieved from https://www.titanfile.com/blog/huwhat-is-data-encryption-and-why-is-it-important/

Arcserve. (n.d.). 5 Common Encryption Algorithms and Unbreakables Future. Retrieved from https://www.arcserve.com/blog/5-common-encryption-algorithms-and-unbreakables-future

TechTarget. (n.d.). Use These 6 User Authentication Types to Secure Networks. Retrieved from https://www.techtarget.com/searchsecurity/tip/Use-these-6-user-authentication-types-to-secure-networks

Auth0. (n.d.). Authentication and Authorization. Retrieved from https://auth0.

com/docs/get-started/identity-fundamentals/authentication-and-authorization

SailPoint. (n.d.). Difference Between Authentication and Authorization. Retrieved from https://www.sailpoint.com/identity-library/difference-between-authentication-and-authorization/

TechTarget. (n.d.). Incident Response. Retrieved from https://www.techtarget.com/searchsecurity/definition/incident-response

Cynet. (n.d.). Incident Response Management: Key Elements and Best Practices. Retrieved from https://www.cynet.com/incident-response/incident-response-management-key-elements-and-best-practices/

The Hartford. (n.d.). Cyber Incident Response Plan. Retrieved from https://www.thehartford.com/insights/cyber/cyber-incident-response-plan

Agility Recovery. (n.d.). Steps to Take After a Data Breach. Retrieved from https://www.agilityrecovery.com/article/steps-take-after-data-breach

LinkedIn. (n.d.). How Can You Communicate with Stakeholders During Cybersecurity Incidents? Retrieved from https://www.linkedin.com/advice/1/how-can-you-communicate-stakeholders-during-cyber

Ahead Intranet. (n.d.). 5 Ways Internal Communication Can Strengthen Cybersecurity in Your Organization. Retrieved from https://www.aheadintranet.com/blog-posts/5-ways-internal-communication-can-strengthen-cybersecurity-in-your-organization

Software Secured. (n.d.). Lessons from Incident Responses. Retrieved from https://www.softwaresecured.com/post/lessons-from-incident-responses

eTactics. (n.d.). Incident Response Examples. Retrieved from https://etactics.com/blog/incident-response-examples

Kiteworks. (n.d.). Security Governance. Retrieved from https://www.kiteworks.com/secure-file-transfer/security-governance/

Critical Start. (n.d.). The Importance of Understanding and Adopting a Cybersecurity Framework. Retrieved from https://www.criticalstart.com/the-importance-of-understanding-and-adopting-a-cybersecurity-framework/

TechTarget. (n.d.). 6 Principles for Building Engaged Security Governance. Retrieved from https://www.techtarget.com/searchsecurity/post/6-principles-for-building-engaged-security-governance

IgnitionIT. (n.d.). Importance of Cyber Security Compliance. Retrieved from https://ignitionit.com/importance-of-cyber-security-compliance-igt/

International Comparative Legal Guides. (n.d.). Cybersecurity Laws and Regulations - USA. Retrieved from https://iclg.com/practice-areas/cybersecurity-laws-and-regulations/usa

Kiteworks. (n.d.). Cybersecurity Risk Management. Retrieved from https://www.kiteworks.com/risk-compliance-glossary/cybersecurity-risk-management/

Global Risk Management Institute. (n.d.). Importance of Risk Management in Cyber Security. Retrieved from https://grm.institute/blog/importance-of-risk-management-in-cyber-security/

Drata. (n.d.). Risk Assessment Methodologies. Retrieved from https://drata.com/blog/risk-assessment-methodologies

Synopsys. (n.d.). What is Security Risk Assessment? Retrieved from https://www.synopsys.com/glossary/what-is-security-risk-assessment.html

Venafi. (n.d.). Top 10 Vulnerabilities That Make IoT Devices Insecure. Retrieved from https://venafi.com/blog/top-10-vulnerabilities-make-iot-devices-insecure/

SISA Infosec. (n.d.). The OWASP IoT Top 10 Vulnerabilities and How to Mitigate Them. Retrieved from https://www.sisainfosec.com/blogs/the-owasp-iot-top-10-vulnerabilities-and-how-to-mitigate-them/

CISO MAG. (n.d.). 10 IoT Security Incidents That Make You Feel Less Secure. Retrieved from https://cisomag.com/10-iot-security-incidents-that-make-you-feel-less-secure/

VMware. (n.d.). Application Security. Retrieved from https://www.vmware.com/topics/glossary/content/application-security.html

Forbes Tech Council. (2020, July 16). 14 Expert Tips for Choosing a Secure Messaging App. Forbes. https://www.forbes.com/sites/forbestechcouncil/2020/07/16/14-expert-tips-for-choosing-a-secure-messaging-app/?sh=2bf2cf604ebf

TechTarget. (n.d.). Identity Access Management (IAM) System. Retrieved from https://www.techtarget.com/searchsecurity/definition/identity-access-management-IAM-system

Cybriant. (n.d.). Security Benefits of Identity and Access Management (IAM). Retrieved from https://cybriant.com/security-benefits-of-identity-and-access-management-iam/

Flower, J. (n.d.). Managing Your Digital Identity: Unlocking the Power of Access. Retrieved from https://www.linkedin.com/pulse/managing-your-digital-identity-unlocking-power-access-joe-flower/

Resmo. (n.d.). Access Control Best Practices. Retrieved from https://www.resmo.com/blog/access-control-best-practices

Delinea. (n.d.). Digital Identities: The Future and How We Will Get There. Retrieved from https://delinea.com/blog/digital-identities-the-future-and-how-we-will-get-there

GeeksforGeeks. (n.d.). Cryptography and Its Types. Retrieved from https://www.geeksforgeeks.org/cryptography-and-its-types/

TitanFile. (n.d.). What is Data Encryption and Why is it Important? Retrieved from https://www.titanfile.com/blog/huwhat-is-data-encryption-and-why-is-it-important/

Arcserve. (n.d.). 5 Common Encryption Algorithms and Unbreakables Future. Retrieved from https://www.arcserve.com/blog/5-common-encryption-algorithms-and-unbreakables-future

TechTarget. (n.d.). Use These 6 User Authentication Types to Secure Networks. Retrieved from https://www.techtarget.com/searchsecurity/tip/Use-these-6-user-authentication-types-to-secure-networks

Auth0. (n.d.). Authentication and Authorization. Retrieved from https://auth0.com/docs/get-started/identity-fundamentals/authentication-and-authorization

SailPoint. (n.d.). Difference Between Authentication and Authorization. Retrieved from https://www.sailpoint.com/identity-library/difference-between-authentication-and-authorization/

TechTarget. (n.d.). Incident Response. Retrieved from https://www.techtarget.com/searchsecurity/definition/incident-response

Cynet. (n.d.). Incident Response Management: Key Elements and Best Practices. Retrieved from https://www.cynet.com/incident-response/incident-response-management-key-elements-and-best-practices/

The Hartford. (n.d.). Cyber Incident Response Plan. Retrieved from https://www.thehartford.com/insights/cyber/cyber-incident-response-plan

Agility Recovery. (n.d.). Steps to Take After a Data Breach. Retrieved from https://www.agilityrecovery.com/article/steps-take-after-data-breach

LinkedIn. (n.d.). How Can You Communicate with Stakeholders During Cybersecurity Incidents? Retrieved from https://www.linkedin.com/advice/1/how-can-you-communicate-stakeholders-during-cyber

Ahead Intranet. (n.d.). 5 Ways Internal Communication Can Strengthen Cybersecurity in Your Organization. Retrieved from https://www.aheadintranet.com/blog-posts/5-ways-internal-communication-can-strengthen-cybersecurity-in-your-organization

Software Secured. (n.d.). Lessons from Incident Responses. Retrieved from https://www.softwaresecured.com/post/lessons-from-incident-responses

eTactics. (n.d.). Incident Response Examples. Retrieved from https://etactics.com/blog/incident-response-examples

Kiteworks. (n.d.). Security Governance. Retrieved from https://www.kiteworks.com/secure-file-transfer/security-governance/

Critical Start. (n.d.). The Importance of Understanding and Adopting a Cybersecurity Framework. Retrieved from https://www.criticalstart.com/the-importance-of-understanding-and-adopting-a-cybersecurity-framework/

TechTarget. (n.d.). 6 Principles for Building Engaged Security Governance.

Retrieved from https://www.techtarget.com/searchsecurity/post/6-principles-for-building-engaged-security-governance

IgnitionIT. (n.d.). Importance of Cyber Security Compliance. Retrieved from https://ignitionit.com/importance-of-cyber-security-compliance-igt/

International Comparative Legal Guides. (n.d.). Cybersecurity Laws and Regulations - USA. Retrieved from https://iclg.com/practice-areas/cybersecurity-laws-and-regulations/usa

Kiteworks. (n.d.). Cybersecurity Risk Management. Retrieved from https://www.kiteworks.com/risk-compliance-glossary/cybersecurity-risk-management/

Global Risk Management Institute. (n.d.). Importance of Risk Management in Cyber Security. Retrieved from https://grm.institute/blog/importance-of-risk-management-in-cyber-security/

Drata. (n.d.). Risk Assessment Methodologies. Retrieved from https://drata.com/blog/risk-assessment-methodologies

Synopsys. (n.d.). What is Security Risk Assessment? Retrieved from https://www.synopsys.com/glossary/what-is-security-risk-assessment.html

Venafi. (n.d.). Top 10 Vulnerabilities That Make IoT Devices Insecure. Retrieved from https://venafi.com/blog/top-10-vulnerabilities-make-iot-devices-insecure/

SISA Infosec. (n.d.). The OWASP IoT Top 10 Vulnerabilities and How to Mitigate Them. Retrieved from https://www.sisainfosec.com/blogs/the-owasp-iot-top-10-vulnerabilities-and-how-to-mitigate-them/

Ophtek. (n.d.). 4 Real-Life Examples of IoT Hacked. Retrieved from https://ophtek.com/4-real-life-examples-iot-hacked/

IoTS World Congress. (n.d.). 5 Infamous IoT Hacks and Vulnerabilities. Retrieved from https://www.iotsworldcongress.com/5-infamous-iot-hacks-and-vulnerabilities/

SecurityScorecard. (n.d.). Best Practices for Securing Internet of Things. Retrieved from https://securityscorecard.com/blog/best-practices-for-securing-internet-of-things/

Bytebeam. (n.d.). Guide to IoT Update Management. Retrieved from https://bytebeam.io/blog/guide-to-iot-update-management/

Infosec Institute. (n.d.). The Growing Importance of Cybersecurity in the IoT Era. Retrieved from https://resources.infosecinstitute.com/topics/iot-security/the-growing-importance-of-cybersecurity-in-the-iot-era/

Waverley Software. (n.d.). Top IoT Tech Trends. Retrieved from https://waverleysoftware.com/blog/top-iot-tech-trends/

Balbix. (n.d.). Addressing IoT Security Challenges. Retrieved from https://www.balbix.com/insights/addressing-iot-security-challenges/

Flare Systems. (n.d.). Types of Threat Intelligence. Retrieved from https://flare.io/learn/resources/blog/types-of-threat-intelligence/

UpGuard. (n.d.). Cyber Threat Landscape. Retrieved from https://www.upguard.com/blog/cyber-threat-landscape

SocRadar. (n.d.). Real-Life Examples of Successful Threat Intelligence Operations. Retrieved from https://socradar.io/real-life-examples-of-successful-threat-intelligence-operations/

Proofpoint. (n.d.). The Vital Role Threat Intelligence Plays in Security Awareness Education. Retrieved from https://www.proofpoint.com/us/blog/security-awareness-training/vital-role-threat-intelligence-plays-security-awareness-education

CrowdStrike. (n.d.). Threat Hunting. Retrieved from https://www.crowdstrike.com/cybersecurity-101/threat-hunting/

GadellNet. (n.d.). Cyber Threat Hunting Tools. Retrieved from https://gadellnet.com/cyber-threat-hunting-tools/

Cybeready. (n.d.). Threat Hunting Tools for 2023. Retrieved from https://cybeready.com/threat-hunting-tools-for-2023

Cyborg Security. (n.d.). 7 Threat Hunting Tools Everyone in the Industry Should Be Using. Retrieved from https://www.cyborgsecurity.com/blog/7-threat-hunting-tools-everyone-in-the-industry-should-be-using/

Cybereason. (n.d.). The Eight Steps to Threat Hunting. Retrieved from https://www.cybereason.com/blog/blog-the-eight-steps-to-threat-hunting

FPA Inc. (n.d.). 8 Traits of a Proactive Cybersecurity Strategy. Retrieved from https://www.fpainc.com/blog/8-traits-of-a-proactive-cybersecurity-strategy

ThreatQ. (n.d.). 5 Best Practices for More Threat Intelligence. Retrieved from https://www.threatq.com/5-best-practices-more-threat-intelligence/

Forbes. (2023, October 11). The 10 Biggest Cyber Security Trends in 2024 Everyone Must Be Ready for Now. Retrieved from https://www.forbes.com/sites/bernardmarr/2023/10/11/the-10-biggest-cyber-security-trends-in-2024-everyone-must-be-ready-for-now/?sh=3e36ae6e5f13

Simplilearn. (n.d.). Top Cybersecurity Trends. Retrieved from https://www.simplilearn.com/top-cybersecurity-trends-article

NordLayer. (n.d.). Evolution of Cyber Threats Over 10 Years. Retrieved from https://nordlayer.com/blog/evolution-of-cyber-threats-over-10-years/

CyberSN. (n.d.). Cybersecurity News: Why Staying Current is Vital. Retrieved from https://cybersn.com/cybersecurity-news-why-staying-current-is-vital/

SageNext. (n.d.). Emerging Cybersecurity Challenges. Retrieved from https://www.thesagenext.com/blog/emerging-cybersecurity-challenges

UC Berkeley Center for Long-Term Cybersecurity. (n.d.). Seven Trends in

Cybersecurity 2030. Retrieved from https://cltc.berkeley.edu/publication/seven-trends-cybersecurity-2030/

Bank of America. (n.d.). Adaptive Cybersecurity. Retrieved from https://business.bofa.com/en-us/content/cyber-security-journal/adaptive-cybersecurity.html

SecurityScorecard. (n.d.). 8 Top Strategies for Cybersecurity Risk Mitigation. Retrieved from https://securityscorecard.com/blog/8-top-strategies-for-cyber security-risk-mitigation/

LinkedIn. (n.d.). Promoting Culture of Cybersecurity Awareness in Your Organization. Retrieved from https://www.linkedin.com/pulse/promoting-culture-cybersecurity-awareness-your-organization/

Made in the USA
Columbia, SC
27 February 2025